MW00884743

THE DARK SIDE OF FRANCHISING

*How to Avoid Being Swindled and Make
an Educated Investing Decision*

*The Book the Franchise Industry
Does Not Want You to Read!*

ROBERT EDWARDS

The terms franchise "consultant", "broker," and "coach" are used interchangeably in this book. While we are hesitant to use the term "consultant", as inexperienced operators often abuse this title, it is a term with which buyers are likely most familiar. Additionally, most "consultants" can't be considered "brokers" in the legal sense unless registered in their state with the governing real estate board. "Coach" has also been used.

Regardless of descriptive terminology, keep in mind that everyone is a "salesperson" in some capacity. Trust no one, do your research, keep your guard up, and learn how to differentiate the genuine from the illegitimate.

DISCLAIMER. This book is written from a general perspective and may not apply to your specific situation. Each investor has unique variables, including their location, budget, operational abilities, and more. Information in this book is provided on an "as is" basis and should not be used to make an investing decision. Always consult with a professional who is familiar with your situation before making a decision.

While great care has been taken to ensure the accuracy of this book, errors may be present. We take no responsibility for any errors or inaccuracies. Additionally, specific projections in this book were made using educated estimates and may or may not be accurate. Numbers used were taken from the companies' most recent franchise disclosures as of January 2020, and may or may not be accurate at the time of reading.

The names of characters and companies used in the initial chapters are fictional.

TABLE OF CONTENTS

INTRODUCTION

Ten years ago, I, along with dozens of optimistic investors, lost substantial amounts of money to a franchise.

The opportunity looked failureproof. The business was in the trending organic food sector, it saved customers time and money, and the model had been proven locally in-house for over a decade. All that remained was expanding it across the nation.

At the time, I considered myself to be reasonably business savvy. I had started several successful businesses, worked as a consultant providing business strategy to startups, had read all the right books, and taken all the right courses. Yet there I was, alongside dozens of unhappy investors, equally as out of pocket as them.

When the franchise imploded, shortly after its widely publicized national launch, I thought to myself, "If I, as a reasonably well-versed business expert, can't spot a bad investment, what hope does the general public have?"

It was a sobering thought. In a world where thousands of franchises are bought and sold every year, not a single support structure existed to help investors make better decisions. But why was that? Every other industry provided support structures except for franchising.

Buying a house? Call a realtor. Need insurance? Call a broker. Need a job? Call an executive recruiter. Buy a franchise? Good luck!

Every one of these mature industries provided established groups, industry experts, and infrastructures that gave buyers at least some level of guidance and direction. Franchising, however, was like a vast ocean (or swamp?) with no lifeguards, no rules, no support, and no checks or balances in place to counter the endless sales hype that spewed continuously from franchise sellers.

That simple thought began my journey towards devising a systematized process that would help investors make better decisions and avoid common mistakes. Over the following years, I worked with dozens of entrepreneurs, franchise experts, and even psychologists towards finding the "special sauces" inherent in making quality franchise-buying decisions.

As I studied the industry in greater detail, I was shocked to uncover the level of sleaziness and outright fraud perpetrated on an unassuming public. This book reveals the scammy tactics employed by unethical franchise companies, big and small, which are used to extract millions from inexperienced buyers.

As I began to write this book on January 1 2020, fraud, misrepresentation, lies, and unethical behavior still ran rampant throughout the industry. The internet allows any franchise, regardless of size, to mass advertise to the public at low cost while hiding their poor business model behind a veneer of credibility, which is provided by the industry as a whole.

And while there are undoubtedly good franchises available, and many of us on the Franchise City team have owned and do own them, there is also an increasing number of terrible franchises that ultimately reflect very poorly on the entire industry.

Had I access to the information in this book back then, I would have likely dodged a costly bullet.

Today, I am proud to say my associates and I have helped hundreds of aspiring entrepreneurs make cautious and educated choices. Our company provides a comprehensive suite of completely free tools and services ranging from skills assessments, comparative analysis, red flag reports, and mentorship from highly experienced entrepreneurs around the country. Our YouTube channel, one of the few that delivers a critical analysis of franchises, provides counter-balance arguments and reasons why you may actually *not* want to invest in a particular franchise.

I am incredibly thankful for the social media platform as it has allowed us to forewarn thousands of people against making hasty and potentially disastrous decisions based on nothing more than emotionally charged sales hype.

Much of what is revealed in this book will be off-putting. The predatory tactics employed by unethical operators in the franchising industry are alarming.

Companies blatantly lie to buyers by inflating earnings, using manipulative marketing techniques, and "fear of loss" sense-of-urgency ploys. Some of these tactics are illegal and all are unethical, but there are simply not enough enforcement resources available to address them all. Your best defense as a buyer is an education and a critical mind.

Unfortunately, human beings are emotional creatures. We hear what we want to hear. Over the years, our team has cautioned many entrepreneurs against "can't lose" franchises. And of the "hot deal" de jour that placed highly in an industry "top list". Sadly, caution and restraint are often no match for promises of wealth and easy money. The result? Yet another aspiring entrepreneur added to the ever-increasing list of those who have lost their money and their dreams.

But it's not all bad. Many people have built successful businesses and created wealth by owning a franchise. The business model itself is brilliant, and there are many great franchises. While caution is imperative, it shouldn't equal negativity or avoidance. Admittedly, after reading the following pages, it would be easy to write off the franchising industry as a high risk, poorly regulated haven for scammers and money-hungry profiteers. And sadly, much of it is. But not all.

Like any other industry, there is good, bad, terribly bad, and exceptional.

Unfortunately, it is challenging for the general public to tell them apart. Little real data is publicly available to help investors make a decision based on facts and hard numbers. The same offenders in the franchise industry all play off each other, self-validating how risk-free the franchise model is. Neophyte buyers naturally gravitate to businesses that loudly proclaim the highest profits and most effortless operations. Ironically, companies that shout their praises the loudest, spending heavily on digital marketing, are often those that offer little by way of a viable business model. First-time buyers with no clue of how to identify quality versus shady franchises are lured to their financial dooms with these slick promises of easy six-figure riches.

Conversely, quality franchises will often choose to advertise more conservatively, preferring to partner with a select few franchisees who suit their ideal profile. Their promotions are cautious and realistic, preferring to focus on recruiting the ideal candidate rather than shouting about the magnificent wealth to follow if the investor only signs up today.

As you read this book, keep in mind that scattered among the hundreds of bad-to-mediocre brands, there are indeed good (and great) franchises. If chosen wisely and cautiously, a franchise can provide a healthy partnership between two parties that share a mutual goal.

The first part of this book focuses on the franchise industry's negative aspects and educates buyers on the often slimy tricks employed by unethical franchises. And while we would rather not have to dwell on the negative, buyers must understand the deceptions of which they need to be wary. We will demonstrate how the players within the franchise industry work in tandem with the media to persuade, trick, and cajole buyers into making often disastrous decisions.

Hopefully, one day, franchising will join the twenty-first century in regulatory oversight, alongside industries such as real estate, insurance, and financial services. Until that happens, it is buyer beware.

Once we have covered the proverbial dark side of the industry, the second half of the book concentrates on the positives of franchising. We offer practical strategies towards selecting and vetting your franchise and making an educated buying decision.

We'll explore the top mistakes buyers make when choosing a franchise, how to avoid them, and more. We'll also cover the average earnings of franchises in several industries,

When done right, franchising will provide you with an established business model, a recognized brand, and the support and training to help you build a big business.

When done wrong, it often results in heartache and financial disaster.

Let's learn how to tell them apart!

CHAPTER ONE

THE PROBLEM WITH FRANCHISING

On July 17 2019, a little-publicized presentation was made to the United States Senate Committee on Banking, Housing, and Urban Affairs Subcommittee on Economic Policy.

The presentation entitled "Economic Mobility: Is the American Dream in Crisis?" was penned and presented by Mr. Keith R. Miller, a franchise owner and principal of Franchisee Advocacy Consulting.

In his presentation, Mr. Miller laid out what he called "the good, the bad and the ugly of franchising", and over the next several minutes, listeners were introduced to a welcome rarity in the franchising industry – the truth.

Miller opened his presentation with the assertion that franchising is unquestionably a successful business model that has helped thousands of entrepreneurs become financially successful. Himself included.

What followed was a darker reality that the franchise industry would undoubtedly prefer not to come to light. Miller spoke of the remarkably high number of franchise failures and coercive tactics franchisors often use to lure the unsuspecting public. He spoke of unacceptably high failure rates, figures which were far in excess of any available to the general public.

According to a report referenced in the presentation, of 160,000 franchises opened over a five-year time period, *an incredible 130,000 had closed during that same time!*

Lack of regulation and oversight on behalf of the government was also addressed, and specific examples were given of aspiring investors whose American Dream had turned into a nightmare after being hooked by the hype of franchising.

And this revolving door carries on with the government's blessing, as their Small Business Administration (SBA) programs continue to fund high-risk franchises. They're setting them up to fail.

Anyone outside the franchising industry might find this shocking, but it's nothing new to those within it. We've been cautioning buyers for years, but our advice often falls on deaf ears.

Let me give you an example. In 2014, we began warning buyers against a major fast-food franchise. We believed the company had management problems, placed excessive operational demands on franchisees, had shrinking average earnings per unit, and had reached a market saturation point due to decades of unbridled growth.

Some listened. Others did not. After all, who were we to question one of the most successful brands in franchising history? This was a billion-dollar-a-year corporation that was highly visible on TV, radio, and billboards on every street corner in every city. They were big time, and many people believe – wrongly – that if a company is big, it must be good.

So, in many cases, our concerns were shrugged off. Buyers continued to pour in their hard-earned money and other followed. The theory? Why would so many people invest if the opportunity is not sound? But, much like stocks, real estate, Bitcoin, and other investments, things tend to heat up right before the decline.

And then it hit. The following year saw hundreds of closures. The next year, even more. Thousands of stores eventually shut, taking with them the livelihoods of their investors and plunging them into unfathomable amounts of debt.

Years later (yes, *years* later), the media began covering the story. At last, (rational buyers at least!) began to realize that just because you see a location on every street corner, it does not necessarily mean that *you* will make a ton of money as a franchisee.

Today we receive almost no inquiries about this franchise. Five years ago, a large percentage of our calls were dedicated to that one brand. During this peak period, before the honest media coverage, hundreds of people invested and, as we've noted, some lost everything, while many others continue to struggle to this day, having simply "bought themselves a job".

And this was just one franchise, among hundreds of franchises that combined, sell thousands of opportunities every single year.

The scary part is that this was not even a particularly "bad" franchise. They play by all the rules, and they don't misrepresent or exaggerate. But like most franchises, *they told people what they wanted to hear.*

First-time buyers don't know how to determine if a franchise is good or bad because they lack the context of all the other franchises. They don't know what they don't know.

And what they don't know is this. Is $420,000 a year in gross revenue good? What is a good number for average expenses, margins and net profit? What is the long-term outlook for a brand? What on Earth is a SWOT analysis? (Clue: it's less about obliterating flies and more about determining the strength, weakness, opportunity and threat of a particular business.) Could other franchise options earn me more? Are my skills and operational preferences in alignment with the day-to-day demands of the franchise?

Sadly, for first-time franchise buyers, there are not many places to turn to for advice on what questions to ask, and where (and where not) they should put their money. Many will consult industry "top lists" or franchise books which, as we will demonstrate in a later chapter, are often, at worst, pay-for-placement PR, or at best, ridiculously inaccurate.

Most other mature industries, such as insurance, real estate, and financial services, have at least some level of support available through professional groups, all regulated by some level of oversight and code of conduct. In franchising, there are no regulated entities to engage. In fact, the lack of regulation in the industry allows anyone to call themselves a "franchise consultant" and advise buyers on how they should invest hundreds of thousands of dollars!

Think about that for a moment. Someone could be an unemployed toaster repairperson on Monday, and on Tuesday choose to call themselves a "franchise consultant". They can then purchase "leads" (names of people who inquired about a franchise on the franchise portals), ply the unwary buyer with promises of easy wealth, and potentially receive a *$40,000 check* by the end of the month.

Yes, a $40,000 payout. It is obvious why these enormous payouts can, and do, lead to unethical behavior, particularly when this industry segment has almost no oversight.

Unethical "consultants" and salespeople can, and do, receive five or even six-figure commissions on a single deal simply for referring just one candidate who ultimately purchases a franchise. In the following chapter, we'll reveal exactly how the industry lures unsuspecting victims in, circumvents existing rules and laws and tricks buyers into signing on the dotted line.

Yes, there are good consultants, coaches, brokers, and franchise groups working hard to make the industry a better place. Many provide a valued service. But the lack of regulation and oversight means unethical operators make up the majority, and this casts a negative light on the industry as a whole.

Competing against unethical consultants is difficult. While our message to a candidate is one of restraint and caution, immoral brokers boast of guaranteed wealth with minimal effort. You don't need to be a genius to see why our sensible but dull warning is often the one people will push aside.

And don't for a second think it's only the naïve candidates who get conned. The franchise industry uses a very slick methodology to authenticate its misrepresentations and exaggerations over multiple levels to circumvent what little effective regulation has been put in place to protect consumers.

In fact, the entire industry, from top to bottom, self-validates to such an extent it makes anyone with a critical message look like a "Debbie Downer". It is not the American way to be cautious or analytical; just jump in and make money!

We currently have over 150 videos on our YouTube channel that illustrate some of the downsides franchise buyers will face. Most viewers are appreciative, but there are also many comments suggesting we are overly "negative". Despite the fact we always include our sources and reference statistics, some people don't want to hear it. They would rather live in a fantasy world than have their dreams crushed.

There is a well-worded paragraph in a book written by Robert Greene and Joost Elffers called "The 48 Laws of Power" that summarizes the state in which some buyers entrance themselves:

"The truth is often avoided because it is ugly and unpleasant. Never appeal to truth and reality unless you are prepared for the anger that comes from disenchantment. Life is so harsh and distressing that people who can manufacture romance or conjure up fantasy are like oases in the desert: everyone flocks to them. There is great power in tapping into the fantasies of the masses."

Unfortunately, this utopian mindset is what has led to the massive numbers of franchising casualties.

Be critical, and don't allow emotions to cloud your judgment. The truth might be ugly, but it could save you thousands of dollars. It could even save your livelihood.

CHAPTER TWO

THE LEGAL CON

Let's begin with a scenario involving a typical aspiring investor who is setting off on her journey to owning a franchise. We'll call her Susan.

Most people start with a basic online search for "best franchises", or perhaps "most profitable franchises", and Susan does the same.

After her search, hundreds of ads, webpages and industry accolades appear, all loudly proclaiming the incredible benefits of franchising.

"Franchising has a 95% success rate!"

"Our franchise was ranked #5 in XXXXX list"

"Featured in XXXXXXXXX publication"

"Chosen as a top 12 franchise for 2020"

"Eight years on the franchise top list"

"Voted a top franchise for veterans"

Wow! The world of franchising looks fantastic. Not just full of opportunities and hitherto-unknown riches, but completely failureproof. Susan starts dreaming of the day she's her own boss, earning a great salary and with the support of a well-known company behind her.

Susan's no fool so she digs deeper. But everywhere she looks, she finds the same positive messages repeated and validated across multiple platforms, many of them well-known institutions and media outlets. Like others embarking on the same journey, her first impression of franchising is that it's infallible.

After reading the unending barrage of messages telling her to get to it, Susan decides to contact not just one, but several franchises directly. Or so she thinks. And so begins the web of illusion in the franchising industry.

The online form you complete requesting to receive more information might go directly to the franchise *if* you found it directly on the franchisor's website. They might be good or bad, depending on who you're dealing with – we'll cover the tactics used by unethical companies in a later chapter.

However, it's more likely that, following your internet deep dive, you ended up on the website of a lead aggregator.

Many of these web "portals" will sell your information to the highest bidder. That might be the franchise itself, or it might not.

In fact, do you recall our hypothetical out-of-work toaster repairman who decided to call himself a consultant? Well he can buy your information!

Selling your information is big business. Money-hungry franchise salespeople, both independents and those working directly for a franchise, pay top dollar for a chance to hock their wares to you. Franchise lead providers sell your information from a low of $30 to a staggering $160 *or more* if you are a high-value candidate. A high-value candidate might be a downsized executive who is seriously considering buying a franchise and has an acquisition timeline of three to six months.

Anyone can place an advertisement on many of these portals. Some portals allow anyone to place an ad for any franchise they want to promote! So you think you are contacting the franchise when you're actually contacting an ex-toaster repairperson. And nothing against toaster repairpeople in general, but ours is rather shady and knows nothing about franchising. We'll call him Harold.

Some independent consultants request permission from the franchise they are advertising. Others do not. The more reputable portals will request written approval from the franchise before posting any advertisements from brokers. Others do not. Some franchises actively encourage brokers to advertise on their behalf. And that isn't *necessarily* a bad thing if the broker is qualified and ethical. As we've said before, not everyone is morally corrupt. But without any signposts to indicate whether the ad is valid or not, the buyer has no way of knowing where their information ends up.

So Susan, our unwary prospect, completes an online form requesting information for the XYZ Yogurt franchise. Her information is then sold to Harold, our ex-toaster repairman, who had placed an advertisement for XYZ Yogurt and several other franchise brands earlier that week. The more brands he advertises, the higher the number of leads he will receive and the greater likelihood of a nice commission.

Because the franchise portal website is getting paid $30 *minimum* for each lead, they don't want Susan to end her search with XYZ Yogurt, so she's encouraged to complete more forms.

The website bombards her with messages such as: "Did you like XYZ Yogurt? Why not request information for ABC Burgers? Did you like ABC Burgers? Why not request information on EFG Cakes?"

Visitors like Susan are heavily incentivized to complete as many information request forms as possible. Their information is then sold to multiple parties, ranging from the franchise companies themselves to independent brokers and consultants.

And Harold.

After completing several requests for information, Susan expects to receive details by email the next day from these companies, which she can then read at her leisure.

What actually happens is a stampede of hungry franchise salespeople, all of whom just paid $30 or more for her details, call and text Susan as quickly as humanly possible in the hope they will be the first to speak with her.

Obviously, being the last in a long line of annoyingly desperate callers is not a good place to be.

If Harold is glued to his phone or his email, sitting in his rundown apartment waiting for this very lead, he could be the first to call Susan. And he will be waiting. According to industry best practice, portals advise calling your "leads" as quickly as possible.

And this used-car selling, ambulance-chasing modus operandi is often people's first introduction to the world of franchising.

Within moments of completing her online request, Susan gets a phone call (after all, she may not see the email straight away, but it's less likely she'll miss her phone ringing).

"Hi Susan, this is Harold Smith returning your call regarding XYZ Yogurt. How are you today?"

Susan doesn't want to be impolite. She did request the information after all.

"Fine, thanks."

Small talk ensues. "Rapport building" as it's called in the business.

"Let me ask you a question Susan. I know you inquired about XYZ Yogurt, but I work with dozens of franchises, not just XYZ, and I can help you find the best one suited to your specific needs," says Harold helpfully. "Can we discuss your goals?"

Susan learns that, just like working with a real estate agent, the service provided is free. Harold receives a "small" referral fee if Susan buys a franchise. There is no charge to Susan and, therefore, no risk.

Or so she thinks.

And here is where the road diverges. The person at the other end of the phone could be a highly experienced franchise consultant or coach with years of experience, formal training, and a long list of satisfied prior clients.

Or it could be Harold.

Susan decides to move forward. It is, after all, no charge to her. At worst, she figures she will expand her options, learn something new and, as Harold has stressed, she can always say no.

After determining Susan's financial ability, location, goals, and a few other details, Harold concludes the call. He says he will have some recommendations based on her business interests in the next few days.

Here again is where the road can diverge. Harold might be a qualified consultant doing proper research, analyzing Susan's skills, strengths, exit strategy, and other criteria, or he could just be an ex-toaster repairman with no relevant experience preparing to hard sell a single franchise.

The one that pays him the most commission, of course.

Just yesterday, Harold made a special deal with the XXX Burger Franchise corporation. They will pay him a $40,000 commission if he finds a buyer. Keep in mind that most less-than-ethical franchises can, and do, work with anyone who calls themselves a broker, consultant, or coach and will offer massive sums to sell their poorly performing junk. They may offer up to 100% of the franchise fee. We'll learn why later.

So even though Susan was interested in XYZ Yogurt, Harold emails glossy brochures to Susan that cover all the high points of the franchise and outline all of the "top lists" in which XXX Burger has been recently featured. He tactfully avoids any negatives that might turn Susan away.

The truth is, Harold couldn't tell you the negatives even if he wanted to because he doesn't know what they are. Frankly, he doesn't want to know what they are.

Harold points out the benefits of being your own boss and the absolute certainty of success in franchising. In fact, did she know franchising has a 95% success rate? And best of all, XXX Burger franchise locations are making a fortune!

Harold says that Susan would make a great addition to the franchise team, but she'll need to fill out an application form to be considered as a franchisee.

"No hurry," he tells Susan. "But keep in mind two other buyers are also looking at the franchise in your territory!"

Vying against other interested parties for a single territory creates a sense of urgency and is a common ploy in franchising. There might actually be other interested buyers, or there may not be.

Harold then points out that he (as an expert) wouldn't invest in XYZ Yogurt as they have been experiencing troubles in the industry. Harold alleges that as an industry "insider", he has access to information Susan does not. XXX Burger is the way to go.

The fact is Harold has no idea about the financial stability of XYZ Yogurt. He doesn't know how to read financials, and even if he did, it wouldn't matter as he doesn't know where to find the franchise disclosure documents (FDD) anyway.

Harold is lying, plain and simple, to lead Susan towards his desired outcome. A higher commission.

XYZ Yogurt pays Harold a commission of "only" $20,000, half of what XXX Burger offers. Because there are no regulations or background checks for franchise consultants, Harold and his unethical peers can act with reckless disregard towards their "clients".

It is easy at this point to suggest that no one would be sufficiently naïve to fall for these tactics. And while that may be true up to this point, *this call is only the beginning in a long line of deceptions to follow.*

Susan certainly isn't naïve and nor is she stupid so, once the call has finished, she starts to do her own research to reinforce Harold's claims.

Seemingly, the more research Susan does, the more it appears that Harold was telling the truth.

XXX Burger is mentioned prominently on several top lists.. A couple of these are reputable lists from major media outlets.

There are also dozens of press releases covering new locations opening, and references to how quickly XXX Burger has been expanding across the nation. Images of these shiny new stores fill Susan's mind, and she starts to feel excited. This dream might actually be real! She could own her own business! She could be earning a great living while making customers happy!

Not only that, but XXX Burger was also featured in the best-selling book "Great Franchises to Buy in 2019", written by a multiple best-selling author with dozens of books on the market and over three decades of experience.

Susan does several days of research, seeing nothing but positives. Every source she finds online, without exception, speaks to the strong growth, innovative company management, and the bright future of XXX Burger. She doesn't find a single complaint or negative review.

The books, the top lists, the media hype, everywhere Susan looks confirms what Harold has told her. XXX Burger is a brand in which she should invest. Absolutely. No question.

Susan's desire builds, as does her concern of losing the in-demand territory to the two other candidates.

Armed with all this information, which Susan feels has been quality research, she decides to "interview" for the privilege of owning an XXX Burger location. Harold sets up the calls, and Susan begins to work directly with the franchise.

The XXX Burger representative (possibly the franchise owner or a commissioned salesperson) validates all the information given to her by Harold and all the information she has seen online.

"We are growing like crazy," he says. "It is an exhilarating time to be joining."

Because, as we've noted, Susan is not naïve and is far from stupid, she remains cautious and wants to be more diligent. She calls a couple of existing franchise owners (names provided by the company), and is reassured as they seem quite happy. This venture continues to look exceptional, and so she starts the franchisor's formal application process.

A few "interviews" and applications later, she is told by the franchise, "I think we can make this work! Keep your fingers crossed while we wait and see if you are accepted!"

Susan waits for several days. Those days are hellish, full of fear that her dreams are hanging in the balance. What if one of those other two applicants beats her to it? She fantasizes about how great it would be to own a franchise. Images of happy customers lining up next to an overflowing cash register while the sun shines through the restaurant windows fill her mind.

Even if Susan were to read or hear anything negative about XXX Burger at this point, her emotions would likely continue to carry her forward. She's committed.

Thousands of investors, armed with little more than a hopeful vision, decide to become their own boss. Many of them ultimately regret that decision and kick themselves for not being more analytical. If the franchisors would allow buyers to speak publicly of their experiences, and if the media would cover more negative outcomes, buyers might be more cautious.

But that simply does not happen. Buyers will never hear about the vast majority of franchise horror stories. More on that later.

Credit checks completed, applications approved, and, after a nerve-wracking two weeks, Susan gets the call.

"Congratulations Susan! Your application was approved. Welcome to the XXX Burger family."

With a mixture of excitement and no small amount of fear, Susan releases the funds to the franchise (probably in the range of $250-$500,000) and starts setting up her location. Her dream of successful business ownership has finally come to fruition.

Or so she thought.

Business is slow at first. Susan's XXX Burger rep tells her not to worry.. Things will pick up.

By the third month, Susan is still spending more money than she takes in. Calls to corporate start to go unanswered.

By the sixth month, Susan is desperate. The company advised her that she needed only three months of working capital before reaching profitability, but that hasn't happened. The company keeps telling Susan she "isn't following the system" and suggests it is her fault. She needs to give better customer service, hire better people, work at the shop more.

But she is already working twelve hours a day, six days a week. She can't afford to hire more than her existing skeleton staff and she's already working for free herself. Local employment is tight, and it's very hard to find good people at minimum wage, but she can't afford to pay more. She keeps losing employees and struggling to rehire. Susan didn't have any hiring experience, and the training she received didn't help much.

Because her employee turnover is a revolving door, and because XXX Burger's training on hiring and retaining employees was not up to par, her franchise starts receiving negative reviews online. As these increase, fewer and fewer people visit her franchise.

Nine months after her grand opening, with no return calls from the franchisor and with the last of her remaining funds, Susan decides to consult a lawyer.

The franchise lawyer doesn't seem shocked at all. He offers his sympathy and states that her exact scenario, unfortunately, is not a rare occurrence. Susan just got caught up in the extremely unethical, but 100% legal, franchise con.

And the news gets worse.

Susan is responsible not only for all of the money she just lost, which was pretty much all her life savings.

But even if she closes her store and walks away today, *she will be responsible for all of the royalties she would have paid over the next two years!*

Let that sink in. If Susan closes her doors, she is legally responsible for paying the royalties – the fee that the franchisee pays the franchise, which ranges from 4% to more than 12% of the revenue – that she would have generated had the store been profitable.

And if Susan has a spouse, their earnings can also be used, legally, to pay these debts once her own finances are exhausted.

XXX Burger franchise had included a "liquidated damages" clause in their agreement that Susan had missed. It's not hard to miss one sentence of fine print hidden within a 280-page document. Liquidated damages clauses are quite common in franchise agreements and oblige the franchisee to pay any outstanding royalties based on a predetermined calculation if they close their locations for any reason.

If the franchise closes, all those royalties the store would have made become due immediately, in one terrifyingly high lump sum.

While this clause does help protect good franchises from franchisees abandoning the store, it can squeeze every last penny out of unwary investors when used by unethical companies.

Susan is devastated. How did this happen? What about all the positive reviews? The top lists? The books? The famous author? The media coverage?. All of these, without exception, had validated XXX Burger as a great choice, not as a rip off.

And to make matters worse, she was directly lied to! Susan tells the lawyer that Harold lied about how much money she could earn and how well all the other franchises were doing.

Once she had been a franchise owner for a while, Susan spoke with other franchise owners who, like her, were struggling, and many who were closing their doors. She realized that among the promotional material, she had received a company-selected shortlist, a minority franchise list of the select few locations that were doing well. The potential revenue was an outright lie – as was the story of low failure rates and systemwide growth.

On hearing this, the lawyer points out to Susan that she had signed an "acknowledgment clause" in the franchise agreement, confirming she had not been provided with any earnings claims.

Acknowledgment is a standard inclusion, required by law and found in every franchise agreement. The clause's original intention was to protect buyers by restricting franchisors or their representatives from lying about their earnings.

With someone like Harold, it allows them to lie through their teeth to make a sale, while the franchise itself has no fear of reprisals.

Harold is an independent contractor. The franchise never said anything. If they do get complaints, everything gets blamed on Harold.

But Harold doesn't care.. He has been a consultant for less than a week, and it's certainly worth the risk for a $40,000 payday! Harold's goal is to close one of these deals every month. That will take him to almost half a million dollars a year. And he can do that with relative impunity while wearing his pajamas.

So what if he has to bend the truth a little.

And right now, there are Harolds all over the country.

In addition to all the Harolds, there is an even greater number of well-intentioned "consultants" who, while not as malicious as Harold, do nothing more than regurgitate what they have been told by the franchises they are selling.

They won't directly lie, but they also won't tell you what you need to know concerning any negatives. What are the failure rates? Industry challenges? Demographic alignment? Is the franchise suited to your local market demand? These are just a few of the things buyers need to know to make a quality decision. And these are the types of things to which an experienced and genuine consultant will draw your attention.

First-time buyers simply don't know what questions to ask or what they need to look for. And an unethical consultant isn't going to bother raising those questions for them.

Because despite basically being nothing more than a walking sales brochure, these consultants/coaches/brokers retain tens of thousands of dollars in commission by leading buyers like Susan up the garden path.

Unfortunately, franchising is one of the last remaining industries where pirates are still allowed to operate.

Franchisors are supposed to list any third parties' names representing them in the FDD, yet they seldom, if ever, do. Does the government have time to go after them? No.

Nobody enforces these rules. Occasionally, if a franchisor steps way, way out of line, they will be charged. But there simply aren't enough resources to police the behavior of every single franchise.

It would be relatively easy to require all consultants to receive training on these points and create a code of ethics. Real estate agents have this. Insurance has this. Why not franchising? They wouldn't have be trained to the level of a franchise lawyer, and they wouldn't ever counsel, but instead, point out aspects of the disclosures to which buyers should pay particular attention. Consultants wouldn't be a replacement for the franchise lawyer, but an added layer of diligence alerting buyers to potentially risky elements of the FDD or problems with a franchise that might warrant heightened scrutiny.

If this level of oversight happened tomorrow, and loopholes closed for shady franchisors, hundreds of costly nightmares could be prevented every year. When the buyer has access to *all* the information, bad franchises could no longer be sold, and good franchises would shine even brighter.

But we're not there yet. So today, hundreds of franchises, from horribly bad to mediocre, are sold using tactics that intentionally obscure the negatives of investing in these businesses. Buyers don't know what they don't know, and subsequently, thousands of people every year are chewed up and spat out by the relentless franchise machine.

Susan, emotionally drained, financially destitute, and now in tears, vows to get even. She tells her lawyer she will go to the press, leave bad reviews online, and do everything in her power to warn others from making the same mistake.

The lawyer reminds her she signed an NDA, a non-disclosure agreement that threatens severe financial penalties if she reveals any information about XXX Burger.

The fact that the company is ripping people off is considered proprietary information! Public posts can also be considered libel, and Susan herself could be sued for additional damages.

Susan is now broke, and the company has all of her money, as well as the money belonging to countless other franchisees, so it is much better equipped to fight her in the courts, even if she can prove fraudulent misrepresentation.

Ultimately, the franchise takes over Susan's location for pennies on the dollar, and resells it to the next unsuspecting buyer. This activity, known as franchise "churning", keeps failures off the books and has the business categorized as a transfer, not a closure. A location that is sold to a new owner doesn't look as bad as one that has closed its doors. There is a lot of money to be made churning franchises. Buyers should be wary not only of failure rates but also any franchises that indicate a high percentage of locations being transferred.

So Susan got duped. But how? All those top lists, awards, being featured as a top franchise in best-selling books, the press releases, the webinars, the 95% success rate of franchising … everything checked out. How can this happen?

Very easily. Let's take a look.

CHAPTER THREE

SHOULD YOU USE A BROKER / CONSULTANT

Before we wade any deeper into the franchise swamp, let us once again state emphatically that there are good franchises out there. There are also good consultants, coaches and brokers. We like to think we are in that group. The problem is that to a first-time buyer, it is almost impossible to tell the good from the bad.

Both have exciting stories, both have industry validation, and both will want you to apply to be approved. The difference is that good franchises are highly selective, while bad franchises will accept anyone while performing the charade of having you "qualify" to be an owner.

In other words, with a shady franchise, all you need is money and a heartbeat and you're in. They'll still require you to "apply to be approved" but this is merely a psychological prop to make you think that you need to be worthy. Bad franchises make you believe that only the best of the best are accepted. This ploy also increases the desire and anticipation while the candidate waits to be "accepted".

Good franchises and consultants will also require an application. Many will also ask you to complete a skills or psychometric profile assessment. In their case, they actually use these tools to ensure you are a good fit.

As a consultant, I am highly encouraged when a franchisor rejects a candidate. It's a bit hard on the buyer's ego, but in the long run, it's a far better alternative to failure and loss of their investment.

Good franchises will also withstand the heightened scrutiny we suggest any buyer undertake before signing the contract. We'll cover that later.

Franchising is presented as the best way to avoid failure and gain the support of a national brand.

A cliched and much-overused statement touted by franchisors is that a franchise "allows you to be in business for yourself, but not by yourself".

And *quality* franchising does provide a proven business model with support and training, connections with suppliers, volume discounts, a recognized brand, and a replicable business strategy. But there are far more mediocre and bad franchises than there are exceptionally good franchises.

Thanks to its initial success, franchising has had incredible growth over the past few decades and, at the same time, it's attracted a growing number of less-than-ethical operators, including consultants, brokers and coaches. As the public has become increasingly comfortable with the franchise model, more companies and individuals have joined in order to grab a piece of the pie.

Selling franchises is big business and represents an obscene payday for everyone involved. When you buy a franchise, the sales representatives alone can earn tens of thousands of dollars on a single sale. To someone like Harold, with no reputation to protect, $40,000 is more than enough for him to lie through his teeth.

The franchise industry presents itself as a "surefire" way to start a business from the very first contact with the consultant. The rabid optimism and business hype typically start right at the broker's, or franchise's first contact. That person is extremely important, and while they have a job to do in convincing the buyer that there is a pot of gold at the end of the rainbow, they're fortunate in that they have help along the way.

For, as we saw, the industry is there to back up everything the broker or franchisor says.

As consumers, we see the apparent validation of franchising's success multiple times on virtually every city block. The market prevalence of franchising lulls buyers into a false sense of security. The assumption is that because so many franchises exist, they must be successful.

But that belief is flawed. Just because a franchise is open does not mean it is successful. Remember the "liquidated damages" clause Susan learned of in the preceding chapter. Franchise owners often can't afford to close. Many of the franchises you see are struggling owner-operators who bought themselves a job.

And a very low-paying job at that.

Most buyers aren't stupid. In fact, they are usually quite intelligent. It is unlikely that more than a small percentage would take what the consultant says at face value. The problem is all the multiple other sources validate exactly what the consultant has said.

Would Susan have been better off without using a consultant? In this case, probably yes, as Harold definitely did more harm than good.

But just like there are good and bad lawyers, doctors and real estate agents, there are also good consultants.

A good consultant can provide significant benefits to aspiring franchisees. They know the industry, they hear the news and rumors and have insider information that the general public does not.

Quality consultants also have access to hundreds of franchises, not just one. That impartiality is valuable. Even the most ethical franchise company will always speak highly of their own system, and will never suggest other options. A good consultant can help you choose from multiple franchises and will help you find the best one for your particular skills, business goals, market demand, and demographics.

A good consultant walks you through the process, and just like using a real estate agent, can provide tremendous value. If you work with an experienced (and ethical) consultant, they could well save you from losing hundreds of thousands of dollars and help you find a profitable franchise that you will enjoy operating.

But how can you be sure the consultant you are working with is reputable?

In an ideal world, there would be a governing body that trains consultants while holding them to a common standard of ethics. Just like realtors, an agent would receive severe penalties if they ran afoul of the rules.

Unfortunately, franchising is set up in such a way that it allows consultants, franchisors, and all those involved to push the envelope of impropriety with almost zero risk of repercussions.

As we learned in the previous chapter, the players all know exactly what they need to say to stay within the law, knowing they are legally absolved once you sign the acknowledgment clauses and an NDA.

But just because there are bad personal trainers out there doesn't mean you should avoid going to the gym. An experienced broker, consultant, or coach can provide real value to a first-time franchise buyer.

Let's explore the confluence of events that led our fictional buyer, Susan, to her financial doom and see what she could have done about it.

Firstly, it's easy to think Susan was gullible for not asking Harold for more information regarding himself or his experience. But because of the informality of the first phone call, most buyers don't bother asking for credentials because they aren't aware of the extent of influence this random person on the phone will yield.

At the inception of the relationship, most people expect this consultant will do nothing more than email an assortment of brochures and introduce them to the franchise companies. The process is smooth and designed never to raise any red flags. But you need to be prepared.

Some consultants won't even identify themselves correctly, leaving the caller to assume they work directly for the franchise.

Always ask the person on the phone who they are and what their relationship is with the company.

If they do give you the consultant pitch, claiming they can provide expertise in helping you find a franchise, ask them how. What is the process? Is the consultant formally trained? Can they provide references and testimonials? How many years of experience do they have? A good broker or consultant will provide their background, and any written proof, without hesitation. Many good consultants and brokers come from corporate environments themselves, and many are, or have been, franchise owners.

Our company, Franchise City, only accepts brokers who have extensive franchising and business-ownership experience. Many of us have spent 30+ years building professional reputations that we certainly don't want to risk. A good consultant with an extensive business history will not want to destroy their reputation for the sake of a single deal.

A consultant should also have received training from an industry-recognized group. And while industry training does not guarantee a quality consultant – just like medical school doesn't guarantee a good doctor – it does demonstrate a level of commitment on the part of the consultant. Sadly, there are several "broker mills" that churn out poorly trained consultants for a fee.

In this day and age, it's relatively easy to research your consultant through LinkedIn or other web-based channels. No history at all? Definitely a red flag.

It should be noted that even if the buyer finds a consultant with decades of experience, they should never rely on trust alone. If your consultant offers up nothing but "fantastic opportunities" run the other way. You need to hear both the good and the bad to make an educated decision. No franchise is without challenges. You need to know what those are to determine if *you* are up to the challenge of overcoming them.

Franchise City provides industry reports and data that help buyers make an educated decision. We also create personalized comparative analysis reports that enable buyers to compare multiple brands side by side. Hard data and statistics don't require trust. The facts speak for themselves. And a good consultant or broker will help you understand how to uncover the numbers the bad franchises don't want you to hear about.

So yes, we need to vet our consultant or broker to a higher degree.

But what about everything Susan did *after* she spoke with Harold? Every source, *without exception,* validated what he had said. The top lists, the websites, the media. How do they continue to make misleading statements that lure people to financial collapse?

CHAPTER FOUR – PART 1

THE VALIDATORS: TOP LISTS

As part of her due diligence process, Susan consulted several of the industry "top lists". These lists are highly popular and rank franchises based on various criteria.

The "fastest-growing" franchise in a specific vertical market, for example.

As we saw, XXX Burger was included in several of these lists, including one very prestigious list from a highly reputable media outlet.

You can't blame Susan for taking these at their word. After all it's there in black and white. But if she had looked a little closer at some of these lists, she would have seen that written in tiny print on some of the company websites were the words: **"may receive compensation from companies listed"**.

That's right. To appear on many of these top lists, the franchise company needs to do nothing more than *pay a fee* to be validated as the "fastest-growing burger franchise".

Industry self-validation is rampant. And while unethical, it is not illegal, provided the companies include a disclaimer. Several online lists will include anyone and everyone who pays.

The lists provide instant third-party endorsement for any franchise that will spend the money. And because they disclose the relationship (in fine print that most people don't read), they are free to continue year after year, supporting the sales hype that people like Harold are spouting, and fooling buyers into parting with their cash.

But what about lists from reputable media companies such as Entrepreneur magazine?

XXX Burger was on there as well (hypothetically, of course).

Franchise companies like to shout this particular ranking from the rooftops. "We made the Entrepreneur Franchise 500®again!"

They add the Franchise 500® badges on their websites as if somehow this media company has endorsed them completely, and buyers need nothing more than to trust these industry lists to make a wise decision.

Buyers eat it up. They love the list. And sure, it is fun to read. However it is truly disheartening to see people using inaccurate information to make a financial decision. But they do.

We have demonstrated in multiple videos on our YouTube channel how many terrible franchises end up on that list.

Franchises with multiple lawsuits. Franchises with high failure rates, franchises with terrible buyer satisfaction, even franchises that have been convicted of fraudulently misrepresenting statistics.

The reality is there is simply no way to vet hundreds of franchises every year to the extent required to build an accurate top list.

What most people fail to acknowledge is that Entrepreneur magazine is a *media outlet*. Not a franchising company. They make money from publishing the list. The more eyeballs on their list every year, the more money they make. They also license their badges, and can even generate leads for your franchise company.

Taken from their own website:

Leverage and Enhance Your Ranking

Find your next qualified franchisee with a lead-generating advertising program within Entrepreneur.com's franchise section. Contact: [email removed]

https://www.entrepreneur.com/page/287361

Pretty good business. They control the list, and *for an added fee,* franchise companies can "enhance and leverage" their ranking. Their words, not ours.

Theirs is the single most anticipated list in the industry. If you Google Franchise 500®, you'll see hundreds of franchises proclaiming proudly, "We made the list again!" Some go as far as suggesting that inclusion in the Franchise 500® is proof that buyers are making a wise decision.

All this despite the fact the Franchise 500® states that buyers should *not* use this information to make a decision (in fine print that few people ever read).

They cover themselves with this disclaimer:

All companies are judged by the same criteria: objective, quantifiable measures of a franchise operation. The most important factors include financial strength and stability, growth rate and size of the system. We also consider the number of years a company has been in business and the length of time it's been Franchising, startup costs, litigation, percentage of terminations and whether the company provides financing. Financial data is analyzed by an independent CPA [Chartered Professional Accountant].

Note: **The Franchise 500® is not intended to endorse, advertise, or recommend any particular franchise. It is solely a tool to compare franchise operations.** *You should always conduct your own careful research before investing in a franchise. Read the FDD and related materials, get help from a franchise attorney and an accountant to review legal and financial documents, talk to as many existing and former franchisees as possible, and visit their outlets. Protect yourself by doing your homework to find the opportunity that's best for you. [**Bold by us**]*

Taken from https://www.entrepreneur.com/article/253977

By including this, Entrepreneur magazine has covered itself legally.

It also reveals that the criteria used in the list is not even "store-level" information that would be important to a buyer.

It's high-level information pertaining to the strength of a company as a whole, which is irrelevant to an investor who needs detail on how the location they're interested in buying has performed.

The 2020 list shows "five pillars" that are taken into consideration when deciding whether or not to include a particular franchise:

COSTS & FEES

- Franchise fee
- Total investment
- Royalty fees

SUPPORT

- Training times
- Marketing support
- Operational support
- Franchisor infrastructure
- Financing availability
- Litigation

SIZE and GROWTH

- Open and operating units
- Growth rate
- Closures

BRAND STRENGTH

- Social media
- System size
- Years in business
- Years franchising

FINANCIAL STRENGTH and STABILITY

- Franchisor's audited financial statements

Do you, as a buyer, care if the company provides financing? Should they get extra points for this? And how does a company get points for social media? Some brands on the list have a poor social media presence.

Growth rate? Having an aggressive growth rate can actually be bad for individual franchisees if the franchise can't support it. Years in business? They often include several startups on the list.

The Franchise 500® claims to look at franchise closures and to use it as part of its criteria. Subway is a massive franchise included as number 107 on the latest 2020 list. **Yet Subway has closed over 2,000 stores in the past three years**.

Within that group of Subway store closures were thousands of buyers who lost it all, some of whom had perhaps validated their investing decision using this actual top list.

Baskin-Robbins is #13 of 500 on the list. **It just missed making the top 10.**

Yet Baskin-Robbins franchised stores are **the single lowest-earning franchise on the QSR50** (the top 50 quick service restaurants, or 'fast-food joints' in the nation). You could not pick a lower-earning franchise from the list if you tried!

The QSR50 is an industry list that ranks QSR restaurants using a number of different criteria, including store-level earnings. The average Baskin-Robbins gross annual revenues are $360,000. To put that in context, an average Chick-fil-A grosses over $4 million a year. But the Franchise 500® list doesn't look at individual store earnings. It looks at the earnings of the entire company. Yes, it is established, yes it has been around a long time, yes its finances are very healthy *corporately*. So it made the list.

Buyers see the list and think owning a Baskin-Robbins must be a great investment as it is #13 of 500 brands.

However, the size of a franchise system, the number of years in business, and its overall financials should mean little to an individual buyer. In fact, several very large, well-capitalized franchise organizations just happen to be very good at selling (and churning) franchises. Their single stores do very poorly, and they have multiple closures in their books. Just because a franchise company has millions in the bank and has been around for 10+ years, it bears no relation to what individual franchisees experience.

Entrepreneur magazine doesn't even look at arguably the most important factors that could help a prospective buyer.

Their own website states:

We do not measure subjective elements such as franchisee satisfaction or management style. *The objective factors are plugged into our exclusive Franchise 500® formula, with each eligible company receiving a cumulative score. [**bold by us**]*

So the single most important factor that could, and should, help buyers make a good decision – franchisee satisfaction – is completely ignored!

Several highly placed franchises on that list have extremely low franchisee satisfaction, as well as alarming failure rates, multiple lawsuits and lackluster earnings at a unit level.

Simply put, the most popular list that touches the majority of the largest franchise brands in the world, the one that is used to endorse the quality of an investment, includes some pretty bad franchises.

But who put this highly coveted industry list together? Surely they must have hired franchising professionals to compile the list?

No they did not.

In fact, if you look below the fine print of their disclaimer, at the even finer print showing who created the list, you will see the *research for the entire list was compiled by individuals with zero franchising experience!*

That's right. The two main individuals responsible for compiling what is perceived to be the most important industry list have zero franchising experience.

The first name mentioned is the lead and is a special projects editor at Entrepreneur Media. Her education is a bachelor's degree in English. According to her LinkedIn profile she runs a side business selling domain names.

The second name mentioned is listed online as an "SEO expert and director of ad operations". SEO, for those who don't know, is search engine optimization.

According to his profile, he has more than four years of SEO and marketing experience. There is no mention of any franchising experience.

Consider this. Hundreds of franchises loudly proclaim inclusion on this list as validation of their business. They add their Franchise

500® badge on the front pages of websites, they add it to their literature and they mention it frequently when speaking with candidates. And every year, hundreds of franchise buyers (including Susan) make a decision at least in part based on the validation of the Franchise 500® list.

A list pulled together by an English major who sells domains on the side and an SEO expert with four years' experience.

A list that doesn't even look at franchisee satisfaction, or other critical unit-level metrics, and arguably includes some of the *worst* franchises.

So the list, quite frankly, is utterly useless from the perspective of a buyer. The disclaimer even states *not to use it for making an investment decision.* But did you read that? Probably not.

This list is churned out year after year, and the public eat it up, investing their retirement savings on a "top" franchise that gets ever richer from the ongoing franchise fees. Because the company sells a lot of franchises, they likely qualify for the list again the following year.

Remember the sobering message at the beginning of the book regarding the number of franchise failures? Sadly, this information gets swept under the rug while industry top lists continue to draw eyeballs and, as a result, manipulate buyers into making poor decisions.

Unbelievably, Entrepreneur magazine's Franchise 500® is one of the "better" lists in that they don't blatantly sell spots for a fee. Many other lists do just that. Buyers don't know any better than to attribute a high level of significance to a franchise that somehow ended up on a list. And who can blame them?

Because while any single resource on its own, such as Harold's grand claims, the franchises fake numbers, the industry top lists, and website sales hype, isn't necessarily enough to move a buyer forward, the combination of all these messages often is.

When you add up the seller's claims, plus multiple instances of industry and media endorsement, you get a falsely optimistic picture that often leads to bad decisions.

But what about the last piece of validation Susan used? The book? It was a national bestseller written by a famous author who has been writing the "12 Best Franchises" series for years.

Hold on to your shirt, it gets even worse

CHAPTER FOUR – PART 2

THE VALIDATORS: INDUSTRY BOOKS

There are multiple franchise books available on the market that supposedly assist a buyer in making better decisions.

These books present themselves as an objective analysis of companies based on the expertise of world-renowned authors.

Nowhere in these books does it disclose the reality that most (if not all) of these publications are simply *pay-for-play advertising sneakily hidden in the guise of a book.*

One very well-known author, self-described as "the most published franchise authority in the world", has made a career out of flogging these books. He has developed a system whereby not only is he paid on each copy sold, but the franchises themselves pay him to write the very copy contained in the book!

This type of advertising is in flagrant violation of Federal Trade Commission (FTC) rules that require disclosures of these types of situations in order to protect the consumer. Taken from the FTC's website:

*If there's a connection between an endorser and the marketer that consumers would not expect and it **would affect how consumers evaluate the endorsement**, that connection should be disclosed. [bold by us]*

https://www.ftc.gov/tips-advice/business-center/guidance/ftcs-endorsement-guides-what-people-are-asking

Now you have to believe that people reading a book containing glowing reviews for a franchise would want to know that not only did those franchises pay to be in the book, **but they actually wrote their own chapters!**

But no disclosures are provided, and this practice continues unchallenged, operating in plain sight, to this day.

Only recently were *some* of the books removed from Amazon. We don't know if Amazon took them down after complaints, or if the author himself removed them pre-emptively after a recent exposé shone light on the practice.

For years investors have relied on these books as gospel, with many undoubtedly losing their retirement savings as a result.

Yet the FTC continues to turn a blind eye, as does the franchise industry itself.

If this type of behavior occurred in any other industry, the company would likely be shut down in a matter of days. But because the deception is wrapped in a high-level veneer of credibility, and because franchising is such a cash cow, authorities choose to ignore it.

Think that you couldn't fall for such a scheme? Think again. Let's see why.

Firstly, the author is noted as a PhD, which lends credibility to his writing. Next, he is a renowned "bestseller", which adds additional credibility to his titles. And finally, the forewords to his books are written by several credible industry professionals (that he lists in his pages of course) suggesting that he is an astute franchising expert who has somehow whittled these franchises down from over 3,000 to a select few, and is presenting the cream of the crop as it were.

FOREWORD FROM THE BOOK:

[The author] masterfully compiles and presents a cadre of concepts destined for greatness, providing readers with a qualified funnel from over 3,000 franchise concepts down to 12 that are worthy of consideration.

This was written by another Dr. with a CFE (certified franchise executive) title after his name. He also teaches a franchising course at a well-known university.

These are not individuals one expects to be involved with questionable activities.

And that is the problem – the industry continuously self-validates within its own ranks, at the highest levels, and sees nothing wrong with it.

So we have a highly rated book series, we have a PhD who is a best-selling author, we have multiple Amazon reviews, mostly positive, we have forewords by prominent industry professionals, and we have endorsements by some of the biggest names in franchising.

Why would we *not* believe what is written in this book?

And buyers can't be faulted for not digging any deeper. Why should you have to?

But the fact is this series of book is nothing but paid advertising. Paid advertising that arguably does not choose good franchises at all.

In fact, several of the franchises that were included in the series a few years ago have since been revealed as having issues ranging from abysmal failure rates to legal issues alleging fraudulent misrepresentation.

Unscrupulous sellers, brokers, and franchise companies alike use these books to authenticate their own stories. Franchise companies listed in the books are encouraged to promote their inclusion on their own social media and websites. In conjunction with the industry top lists and media hype, these books are the shiny brown glaze on the bullshit cake that buyers are urged to ingest.

It's no secret to anyone but the public. Those of us in the industry know full well about this scheme.

These books are nothing more than an "advertising platform", available to any franchise company with a good story and some money.

Franchises pay a fee of $5,000 and then literally **write their own story about how great they are!**

For anyone who is confused, here is the summary:

1. Franchise company "applies" and pays $5,000 to be included in a "best-selling" book featuring some of the "best" franchises.

2. Franchise company writes its own chapter extolling the virtues of how great its brand is.

3. Best-selling author and PhD releases the book.

4. Franchise company is advised to ask employees and friends to download the book and leave a great review. This immediately drives to book to "bestseller status".

5. Unknowing franchise buyers purchase the book, often attributing great significance to the fact a franchise has been included in a "bestseller" written by a PhD.

Given the enormity of the situation, you would think this practice would be conducted in secret. It's not even done discreetly!

FROM THE COMPANY'S OWN WEBSITE:

Books Help Sell Franchises!

[Company name] can publish your book and help you reach a wide audience. If your book will be of interest to a small business audience – regardless of the topic – contact [company name] to learn about our publishing and book marketing services.

Get your own customized [title removed] Franchise eBook cover!

When your chapter appears in our book, you get your own customized cover that can be used on your web site, in your blog, with your advertising, etc.

*This is another differentiator for your business . . . **it sets you apart from all the other franchise opportunities and becomes your own unique lead generator.***

*Most of all, it adds credibility to your story! Books sell franchises because books are considered next to sacred . . . **if it's in a book, you know it's true.***

On this page, we've included the customized covers for all of the companies that appeared in our most recent title: **[Bold by us]**

So franchises can simply buy validation in this book for $5,000 and then shout from the rooftops how they were "chosen" for inclusion over 3,000 other brands.

They know they're duping the reader: "Books are considered next to sacred … if it's in a book, you know it's true." And they know it works.

Several testimonials from franchise companies on the author's website confirm the fact that entrepreneurs have used the book to make a buying decision.

Franchise companies that have purchased this service seem unashamed to boast about how it resulted in a "lead" that ultimately invested a lot of money after simply reading a book that is, at best, misleading and, at worst, fraudulently misrepresenting.

Insane? Absolutely. And this practice continues today, seemingly with no conscience or remorse that buyers might use the information to make bad decisions.

Just like in the case of our fictional buyer, Susan.

CHAPTER FOUR – PART 3
THE VALIDATORS: THE "STATISTIC"

If you have been exploring franchises for any length of time you have likely come across this little gem:

According to statistics from the U.S. Department of Commerce, less than 5% of franchise outlets fail annually.

If this statistic were accurate, it would bode very well for your franchise investment. A 5% failure rate is very small, almost insignificant. Given your motivation and future dedication to your franchise, it is unlikely that you would become a member of this minority statistic.

But unfortunately, the statistic is simply not true. Not even close. In fact, it has been proven false on multiple occasions. Franchisors have been advised in no uncertain terms to refrain from using that statistic. Yet they still do.

"The statistic", as it has become known in the franchising world, is quoted on hundreds of franchise websites and is regularly used by salespeople, brokers, consultants, and even franchisors, for no other reason but to create a false sense of security in the buyer.

Google it and you'll find it on multiple websites from franchises and broker groups that are doing nothing less than *lying to you*.

We produced a video on our channel back in early 2018 showing just a few of the actual franchises and groups that were still quoting the statistic. When we last checked, none of them had taken it down. It's been years.

The funny thing is that anyone who has been in franchising for longer than 10 minutes knows "the statistic" is false. In fact, whenever any genuine franchise professional sees or hears it, they give the big eye roll. It's staggering that it is still used. And it's sad that people lose their life savings because of it.

But if the information is demonstrably wrong, where did this 95% success rate for franchises come from in the first place?

Back in the 1980s – yes, way back in the '80s – the United States Department of Commerce contacted approximately 2,000 franchisees. Many did not respond, as it was voluntary, which begs the question "if your franchise was failing, would you care to take the time to complete a government survey?" Probably not.

Which is why only 5% *of respondents* claimed to be unhappy with their decision.

So we don't even have a tightly controlled study to begin with. We have a deeply flawed "survey" that was never intended to validate franchising. Over time that rather flaky statistic became inverted by the salespeople in franchising and became a 95% success rate.

So not a study but a survey that was wholly voluntary, highly inaccurate, and now almost 40 years old is seemingly the best statistic franchisors can provide.

Salespeople, being as creative as they are, banged the heck out of this statistic for years. Variations of that 5% franchise failure rate and 95% success rate permeated the landscape for over two decades. It became so pervasive that the International Franchise Association had to send out a letter in 2005.

Taken from the letter:

Of particular concern is information claiming that the success rate of franchised establishments is much greater than that of independent small businesses. Many years ago, the U.S. Department of Commerce conducted studies about Franchising which presented such statistics. That information is no longer valid. The agency stopped conducting such studies in 1987.

You know things have gotten crazy when the industry's own representative tells you to lay off.

That letter went out 16 years ago, yet we still have franchise salespeople, franchisors, brokers, and "consultants" using it with impunity today. And not just shady back-alley franchises. Some pretty big names still use the statistic, or creative variations thereof. No matter how you present it, the fact is that franchising has a very high failure rate that is getting higher because of all of these shenanigans that are allowed to continue.

So what are the real franchise failure rates? It's difficult to say because even though there are several credible studies, none of them are in complete agreement. Some suggest franchising fails at a higher rate than independent startup businesses!

While that is unlikely, it does indicate that franchising, as an industry, is not providing the surefire success that it boasts about on websites and in books.

However shocking the numbers may be, industry-wide statistics should be meaningless to the buyer. In fact, equally as meaningless as a top list or a book.

Why?

Let's say that franchising did have a 95% success rate. But you invested in a franchise that had a 75% failure rate. Isn't that the number that should concern you?

An industry-wide number provides no relevance to you as an investor. What matters is the single franchise you are exploring. That is the important figure.

So when the false statistic adds to the industry bestsellers written by PhDs, industry top lists created by major publications and optimistic claims from franchisors and their representatives, it makes for a compelling story. And while no single piece of data on its own would necessarily compel a buyer to invest, the combination of all these corroborating sources do.

And hundreds of people lose their life savings every year based on the illusion of franchising's infallibility.

CHAPTER FIVE

THE SALES PROCESS

This chapter will cover the actual sales process and the tricks franchise companies use to coerce buyers into signing on the dotted line.

Every franchise's sales process begins with their advertising efforts, which may include websites, banner ads, Google ads, or network promotions.

It is an unfortunate reality that first-time buyers, with little to no experience, will, in most cases, be attracted to companies with big claims. Topics such as huge earnings, easy operations, quick return on investment (ROI) draw them in.. You see these types of ads everywhere. And the prospective buyer can't be faulted for wanting these things. After all, who wouldn't want an "easy six figures"?

But legitimate, established, and ethical franchises simply don't market this way. You will never see McDonald's touting an advertisement that screams "Earn Millions with Your Own McDonalds", or Taco Bell claiming you can make "Big Bucks with Tacos".

Legitimate and credible brands promote their franchises based on their business model's quality, how they fill a market niche, their longevity and, most importantly, the type of candidate they are seeking. They may make mention of potential earnings in subsequent material, but generally, the information will be positioned subtly. Rarely will they mention money in the headline.

Newer franchises that have little to offer by way of a solid business model, or market longevity, will often use headlines such as "Six Figure Income with our Franchise", or "$200 Per Hour Cleaning Tiles!!!!"

Experienced investors will be put off by these boasts, and identify the companies behind them as questionable outfits. They understand that real franchises don't use headings with multiple exclamation marks (otherwise known as 'screamers') or all-caps proclamations of imminent wealth.

In addition to being unethical, making an earnings claim that is not included in their disclosure is against the law. That said, as stated earlier, there is simply not enough enforcement available to address every instance.

Unless the franchise has an "Item 19" – which is a financial disclosure – listed in its legal documents, it is prohibited by law against making any references towards potential earnings.

The only exclusion to this restriction is in cases where the franchise does have earnings listed in their FDD (the financial disclosure documents for those who have forgotten). It is then legally allowed to publicize those earnings, as long as they match what is in the FDD.

This includes oral, visual, or written representations. So if the advertisement, the salesperson, or their representative tells you something other than what is *exactly* listed in the FDD, it is in contravention of franchise law.

For example, even if the franchisor gives you a vague projection, such as you could make enough to "buy a Mercedes in a year" that is an earnings claim.

Unethical franchises like to push the envelope in this regard. Many emerging brands are tempted to provide the potential buyer with the earnings of their flagship store. So if the company operated its own location for years before it franchised the business, and earned $1,200,000 a year, it's tempting to give people that impressive figure.

It's also tempting if the franchise has one operator in the system doing over a million dollars a year to reference the opportunity as having "million-dollar potential" to interested buyers.

But unless this information is listed in the FDD, it is illegal to disclose it publicly. The franchisor can direct you to speak with the franchise owner who is making the million dollars a year, as the owner is not bound by these rules, but the franchisor, in the absence of an Item 19, is breaking the law if they discuss earnings.

Of course, franchises do say these things. But they aren't supposed to. And if the franchisor you are speaking with does not have financial information listed in their Item 19, but is still telling you how much you can make, that is a red flag. Their lawyer will have almost certainly counseled them not to break the law, and it is highly unlikely the franchisor is simply ignorant of the rules. What is more likely is that they know, but don't care, which should be a big red flag for the buyer.

Don't ignore these red flags or let your emotions and feelings of excitement override them. The time to catch these unethical activities is *before* you invest, not after. Remember how Susan signed an "acknowledgment clause", which stated her decision was made based *only* on information found in the FDD, and that no other claims of any type were made. You'll be signing that clause as well.

In addition to making illegal-earnings claims, many unethical franchisors use various sales tactics and psychological props to trick the buyer into signing on the dotted line.

In a previous chapter, we covered the "application" ruse, where franchises send an application early in the process to see if you comply.

Major franchises often use this tactic. If you contact virtually any major fast-food chain about owning a franchise, it's unlikely that you'll be able to speak with anyone or ask any questions. You'll be told to download an application, and if you complete and submit the form, you might get a call back. It's more likely that you'll have to follow up multiple times before you get a call back.

This tactic works best for the major brands because they have the clout to make buyers jump through hoops to get a reply. Not only does it get rid of time wasters, or "tire kickers" as they're called in the industry, but it also gives the brand the psychological upper hand right at the beginning of the process.

They know buyers must be interested, despite not knowing anything about the opportunity. Why else would they be completing these forms?

And by having you jump through hoops, the franchisor has the psychological advantage. You feel like the heartbroken lover trying to win the affections of the most popular person in the country.

By keeping you in this hoop-jumping mode throughout the process, you are continually filling out forms, "interviewing", and vying for the acceptance of the franchise. It gets you thinking, "this must be a prize worth fighting for, or why would I have to submit so many applications to qualify? I hope I am good enough to be accepted."

Even the franchises with abysmally low earnings per store and thousands of closed locations will make you "qualify" to be an owner. As we've said before, the reality is if you have the cash and a heartbeat, you're in.

But all franchises will have you complete an application at some point. Some sooner, some later. And while in some situations, this hoop-jumping *is* merely a sales tool and psychological prop, with a good franchise, an application is required for genuine reasons – to make certain that you and the franchise are a good mutual fit.

The key to not making a rash decision and jumping into bed with the wrong company, is not to become so emotionally invested that you're fearful of losing the franchise. It is that fear of loss that keeps people filling out the applications and allowing the franchises to intimidate them into signing things without asking any questions.

You are a mere applicant; we are the billion-dollar corporation.

Don't let the franchisor control the process. Ask questions. Engage with the franchisor to learn, to study, and only *if appropriate,* to invest. If the franchisor is too busy to reply to calls now, how do you expect them to act after they have your money?

There are questions you need to know to ask, and only once those questions have been answered can you determine if you even want to own this franchise. Never enter into negotiations that you are afraid to lose. Look for the negatives, ask the hard questions, and don't let the franchisor force you into acquiescence by leveraging their major brand status and power.

Most franchises will, over time, only drip the data you need to make a decision.

Fill out an application – get our brochure. Submit financials – get our FDD. This strategy makes buyers become more engaged with each step and less likely to walk away. If Baskin-Robbins, or any other low-earning franchise, included their earnings at the beginning of the process, how many people would buy?

But there are multiple ways to get this data without jumping through hoops. Calling Franchise City is one of them! There are also ways to purchase FDDs online, and some states store them in online repositories.

Ultimately, you want to own a franchise that considers you to be an equal and is responsive to your concerns and questions. Not a franchise that ignores you and bullies you into filling out applications to be graced with the honor of owning a location.

Smaller franchise brands that do not yield the major franchises' industry clout use different tactics, which often include high-pressure sales.

A good seller will arm you with information and help you to research at your own pace. They will provide full details on the franchise, including the obstacles and challenges you will face as a franchisee. They will respect your timeline and calibrate their sales process to your personality. Some buyers need more facts and figures while others are comfortable with receiving a high level of information. A good seller will have the answers to your questions, whatever they are.

Has the franchisor given you an artificial timeline or advised you that someone else is vying for the same territory? This is a red flag and could indicate a high-pressure sales tactic is being used. Great franchises will never use high-pressure tactics because they want to be sure you are a good match for them, just as much as you want to be sure the franchise is a good fit for you. They will never rush the process.

Although there is a caveat here. If you are looking at a resale business, it is quite possible that there will be multiple buyers. A new franchise has less chance of having multiple buyers. It's not impossible, but it's less likely, unless the franchisor has marketed specifically to that area.

There are many other tactics employed that are not limited to the franchising industry. These ploys have been used forever by everyone ranging from the local used car dealer to the shoe salesperson.

They include playing on your fear of losing a deal, touting time-sensitive, limited-availability opportunities, appealing to greed, feigning indifference, using closed questions to steer you down a predetermined path (do you like coffee? Do you like people? Could you see yourself as an owner of this franchise? Do you think you could be successful?) and many others.

Bottom line, if you feel like you are being pressured or manipulated, don't be afraid to walk away. Almost all the brands that use these techniques do so because they are trying to hide something, are desperate to sell franchises, or both.

Many franchises also hire individuals with a similar background to their prospective buyers, which has the effect of immediate rapport. One of the most heinous examples of this is hiring veterans to sell poorly performing franchises to other veterans.

This tactic has become so pervasive we have dedicated the next chapter to this topic. If you are a veteran or know a veteran who is exploring franchises, this is critical information.

CHAPTER SIX

VETERAN "FRIENDLY" FRANCHISES?

The intent behind franchise-incentive programs for veterans is honorable. It's to provide discounts and incentives to servicepeople enabling them to start their own business.

What we don't hear about is the insidious nature of some of these programs.

Where franchises touted as "veteran friendly" are actually nothing more than con artists posing as the trustworthy franchise partner of veterans and promoting poorly performing junk.

Many franchises, financing companies, and the government provide cash incentives, discounts, and financial benefits to veterans, often helping them save thousands from the franchise fee – which is great. But when our former servicemen and women are being misled and manipulated into making bad decisions, that's not great. We have heard many "off the record" horror stories from veterans over the years who feel they were misled or outright swindled. They're off the record, as many of them fear the legal repercussions if they are caught violating their non-disclosure agreements.

Again, we see the terrible extent that some people are willing to go to line their own pockets. It's bad enough taking the lifetime savings from a civilian, but bankrupting a veteran takes it to a whole new level.

We have also seen veterans do this to their own. Savvy franchisors may hire ex-armed services as salespeople, which creates an instant connection and rapport with the prospective buyer. Sellers know when you combine a "veteran-friendly" franchise with a veteran salesperson you have a potent recipe for making a sale. Creating a warm and fuzzy feeling at the outset of the process makes buyers more comfortable and less critical.

But buyer beware! Trust no one! Put any franchise you look at under a microscope.

That's not to say good franchises don't hire veterans. They do. But don't let your guard down just because you're speaking to someone with a similar background to your own, or they happen to mention their service. That mistake has cost countless veterans, and civilians, millions of dollars.

But why aren't these stories on the front page news? Any media outlet would undoubtedly have a bombshell news story if they went to print with this ongoing scam.

Firstly, as we know, veterans have signed that same non-disclosure that prevents them from telling others they have been misled or sold a bill of goods. Chances are unless you know someone personally who got ripped off, but you'll never hear about it. Some websites have covered this topic, by allowing anonymous comments, and a few tiny media stories exist buried deep in the recesses of the internet. But overall, unless you work in the industry or know where to look, you will be hard-pressed to find any information at all.

The media, in many cases, also has ties to these poorly performing franchise companies.

Do you think Entrepreneur magazine, the originators of the Franchise 500® would print a story on the negatives of franchises? Unlikely. Many media outlets also receive thousands of dollars in advertising revenue from franchises every year. They are also unlikely to bite the proverbial hand that feeds them.

So this massive story of ongoing fraud, deception and franchisee nightmares never surfaces.

As we have covered, there is a significant number of very poorly performing franchises. There is also a significant number packaged as "veteran friendly" and sold based on that designation alone. While the sentiment of offering discounts is commendable, many of these lists need to do a better job of educating ex-service people on the risks and drawbacks of investing. The "veteran-approved" franchise designation, as noble as it may purport to be, may cause more harm than good by luring unsuspecting ex-military into some really terrible situations.

Let's take a look at some of the franchises that are prominently listed as "great for veterans".

7-Eleven is listed as a "veteran-friendly" franchise.

Yet instead of the industry-standard 6% they'll take over 50% in royalties. They also have a large number of lawsuits and unhappy franchisees.

There are currently a record number of 7-Eleven stores for sale, and since April 2018, stores put up for sale by franchisees have increased by more than 314% in Illinois, 95% in California, 84% in Virginia, 60% in Washington State and 39% in New York.

Sales of franchise-owned 7-Eleven stores *more than quadrupled* from 2013 to 2018. These are owners trying to sell their stores.

The National Coalition of Associations of 7-Eleven Franchisees states:

"Corporate management at 7-Eleven, Inc. (SEI) has continued to ignore requests from franchise owners to create a more transparent relationship. At the same time, franchisees are leaving the system, creating a glut of available stores across the nation."

Turnover of franchised stores due to terminations, non-renewals and abandonments doubled from 150 in 2013 to 314 in 2018. Does that sound veteran friendly? I wonder how many veterans are on this list selling their stores because they basically just bought themselves a low-paying job.

Baskin-Robbins is also listed as a great franchise for veterans. As mentioned earlier, at the time of writing, it has the distinction of being the single lowest-earning franchise on the QSR50. Out of the top 50 QSR food franchises, Baskin-Robbins has the single lowest earnings. Over the past three years, Baskin-Robbins has also closed a net number of over 150 stores. I wonder how many of those stores that lost their money were veterans? XXX

General Nutrition Centers (GNC) is listed as vet friendly. Yet it has closed more than 200 stores over the past three years. That's 200 stores where investors lost their money. I wonder how many of those were veterans.

We could go on for many pages noting franchises that have lots of failures, lawsuits, unhappy franchisees, even some franchises with over a *50% failure rate* – and there are several of them! Is having a 50/50 chance of your business failing considered "veteran friendly"?

Marketers know that when you get the warm and fuzzy feeling at the beginning of your search because of the veteran connection, you are likely to be less critical and more friendly with the seller. This is dangerous.

There is also a psychological benefit to marketing products or services to a specific demographic. For example, if I live in New York, and I am an orthodontist who invests in the stock market, when I see an ad for "Ideal Investments for Dental Professionals in New York", I am highly likely to inquire. The more a marketing piece speaks to you personally, the more likely it will resonate and incent you to inquire.

So when buyers see a "Great Franchise for Minority Veterans", and they are a minority veteran, that opportunity speaks directly to them. And unfortunately, the buyer is at a disadvantage from the start. They think "this franchise is made exactly for me", and instead of being critical, they blindly follow through with the process.

To add insult to injury, many of these franchise recruitment firms and franchise companies know this is the case and so continue to hire veterans to sell franchises to veterans. If you recall, franchise salespeople can earn tens of thousands of dollars on a single sale. In some cases, the salespeople may not be malicious or morally bankrupt. In fact, they may not even be aware of the franchise's shortcomings as they have also been deceived by the franchise company's own sales pitch.

Without previous franchising experience, salespeople are unlikely to know where to look for any evidence that is contrary to what the franchisor tells them.

Buyers need to be critical of every franchise and every salesperson, whether they are supposedly good for vets, minorities, or whomever.

Don't restrict your search to one type of franchise. After all, if someone asked whether you wanted a franchise that is supposedly good for veterans and makes $50,000 a year, or one that makes a million and is not on a veteran-friendly list – which would you choose?

Or if there was a veteran-approved franchise where you worked 60 hours a week and another, that wasn't veteran approved, where you could work 30 hours a week for more money, which would you prefer?

When you look at it this way, who cares if it is supposedly good for veterans? You want the most profitable franchise that makes the most sense in your city and that you are most comfortable operating based on your skills.

The sad reality is that a lot of poorly performing brands just use the term "great franchise for veterans" to lure in unsuspecting buyers. If you watch our YouTube channel, you know there is no shortage of franchises that will take your money and give little in return. And despite bogus industry claims such as "franchises succeed at 95%", the reality is that many fail. There are some great franchises out there, but you have to know where to look and align them with your own skills and goals.

As well as some of these franchises' poor performance, there is another factor that should make anyone think twice about the "veteran-friendly" designation.

Are we expected to believe, that out of millions of veterans, every single one has the same goals, skills, and business preferences?

Or that the cities they live in all have the same demographics and market needs?

Or that all veterans have the same exit strategy and business goals? Of course not! Targeting any group, be it ethnic minorities, the L.G.B.T.Q.I.A community, veterans or any other is nothing more than a *marketing ploy* to sell franchises.

The companies claim that because veterans are great at following systems and processes, that makes them great franchisees. And that's true, but if you buy a franchise with bad systems and processes, it doesn't matter if you follow them, you will fail!

Obviously, not every veteran has the same skills, goals, operational preferences, or exit strategy. Just because a franchise is good for veterans doesn't mean it is good in your neighborhood, doesn't mean you will like conducting the day-to-day activities and doesn't mean you will be good at running the franchise. The best franchise will always be the one that is matched to an individual, not a group. Some veterans are good at sales, and some are not. Some vets are good managing people, others are not. Some cities need more fast food, while others do not.

While there are decent franchises designated for veterans, it is advisable not to limit your pool of prospective brands to the veteran-approved list. The diamond you are seeking may not be found there.

Always be critical and always do your research. Never let your guard down even if (especially if) some friendly veteran salesperson slaps you on the back and tells you how rich you will get if you just sign on the dotted line.

CHAPTER SEVEN

GOOD FRANCHISE, POOR ALIGNMENT

There is no "best" franchise.

We have seen how media stories, industry top lists, and best-selling books all work in tandem to create a falsely positive perception for the franchising industry. We know how to avoid the bad franchises, and the tactics used to make bad franchises look good.

In addition to looking out for bad franchises, buyers also need to be equally cautious of buying a good franchise to which they are personally not well aligned.

Just because a franchise is considered "good" does not automatically make it a good fit for you individually. Another major contributing cause for business failures is a misalignment of a person's business goals, skills, and abilities with the franchise.

Each year we speak with dozens of franchise owners who want to sell their business. Invariably, if the franchise itself is not to blame for their lack of success, the most common reasons for abandoning the business are that they either didn't enjoy it or were simply not good at the day-to-day duties to keep it functioning.

Nobody wants to continue running a franchise when they are not good at managing the business, or their staff, or they're performing activities they hate doing. In these cases, many owners opt to sell, often at a significant financial loss.

Every franchise will have varying responsibilities that include a wide array of roles, including store management, inventory control, sales and marketing, local networking, business to business (B2B) cold calling, customer service, hiring and training, and more.

Most new buyers make the mistake of buying based on a franchise name only, or a specific industry, rather than the operational model. The operational model is more important as it dictates what you will be doing day to day.

Business operations and your required daily activities are far more important than a brand name, or what you might be selling. We'll cover this topic again in our chapter "Top Eight Franchise Mistakes".

There are two critical questions you must ask yourself before committing to a particular franchise. Are you good at the types of activities the franchise requires you to perform, and will you enjoy performing those activities? If you are good at what you do, and enjoy these functions, there is a far greater likelihood you will be successful.

Buyers often picture an idealistic image of the business prior to investing. They think of the money, the prestige and making customers happy, and it makes them feel warm and fuzzy. Little thought is given to the challenges they will most certainly face. All businesses have challenges, and buyers need to be aware of what they are before they invest, in order to determine if they are up to overcoming them.

If these important considerations are overlooked, it means that when the doors open to the business a cascade of previously unrecognized responsibilities, ranging from difficult employees, theft and competition to licensing and compliance issues, hits like a tidal wave and overwhelms the owner.

Certain businesses have a much greater need for operators with a greater tolerance for stress. Others have a greater requirement to drive the business forward through the sales initiatives of the owner. Some require excellent managerial and training skills, and the willingness to deal with constant employee attrition headaches. Industries with minimum-wage employees will require you to be continually hiring and firing and training new recruits. Some personalities are just not well suited to dealing with problematic employees.

For example, in a fast-food restaurant environment, many owners who lack tact, diplomacy, and patience will find themselves confronted with what they perceive to be lazy employees, entitled workers, and a generation of people who don't want to work. For some people, this can be frustrating. Frustration leads to anger, the company culture suffers, and the business ultimately receives negative reviews, which shrink revenue. If you are unhappy, your employees are unhappy, which leads to customers being unhappy.

Even if you find a good fast-food franchise, you are unlikely to thrive in that type of business because it doesn't suit your personality. Even the top franchises have low performers in their system.

Conversely, certain personality types can minimize frustrations brought about by employee friction. They can see the employee's side of things, they don't get flustered, and they maintain a positive work culture despite the frustrations.

It is no secret that two different locations within the same franchise system can provide a completely different customer experience based simply on the owner's personality. You only need to look at review sites such as Yelp to see that. Why is one location an excellent customer experience and the other terrible? It usually comes down to the skills and personality of the owner.

Buyers need to drop their ego and be honest regarding their weaknesses, both in personality and business ability. If you do not, it can be a costly mistake.

Some franchise systems are better than others at ensuring franchisees maintain processes and procedures, others not so much. Ultimately it is up to you, the buyer, to determine which business environment is best suited to your personality.

In addition to dealing with employees, another of your major considerations should be the sales efforts of the business. Every business requires sales of some sort. Many restaurants rely on catering to increase revenue.

How do you get catering customers? You pick up the phone and dial!

Many owners had envisioned standing behind the counter waiting for customers to arrive. Instead, they needed to become B2B salespeople. At least if they wanted to make any money. Some franchises rely heavily on catering as a significant source of revenue.

If the business is driven forward by the sales efforts of the owner, are you willing to do what is required? Do you even know what is required? How many cold calls most owners must make daily? What it's like to make these cold calls? How many sales meetings you will have to attend with local businesses?

There is a misconception that businesses such as restaurants simply run themselves.

While some restaurants permit completely passive ownership, margins will be reduced by hiring a manager unless you have a substantial budget. Also, if your manager quits, that business becomes "hands-on" very quickly!

Owning a restaurant is not just sitting at home while your store prints money. You need to know exactly what activities are involved and then determine if these activities are in alignment with your skills and goals.

It may be hard to believe, but the reluctance to perform sales calls has resulted in hundreds, perhaps thousands, of situations where owners have abandoned their businesses rather than pick up the phone.

During the honeymoon phase of franchise exploration, buyers typically develop a narrow fixation on a business's positives. Money, lifestyle, and the prestige of being your own boss. Roles such as cold calling, ongoing hiring and firing, or walking into businesses to develop relationships are often brushed aside or missed entirely, even if the franchisor discloses them.

When the day comes for the fledgling owner to actually have to walk into a local business and strike up a conversation or cold call a complete stranger, procrastination ensues, and they think, "I'll do that tomorrow."

Even if the owner does force themselves to get on the phone, they are seldom successful. A business, just like a job, is not going to be successful if you hate what you do. Conversely, by aligning your franchise purchase with your own operational preferences and skills, you significantly increase your chances of success. Why? Because you'll enjoy it.

Most of the top franchises will take steps towards ensuring that your skills suit their operational requirements. In fact, if you are not considered a good fit for the business, you won't be awarded a franchise. Not surprisingly, it is often these highly selective franchises that become the most successful, as they have internal systems in place to determine which buyers are willing and able to do what is required.

Unfortunately, the odds are against you finding these top companies randomly as many don't advertise. Many of the heavily promoted franchises just hard sell poorly performing opportunities.

Among the thousands of franchises, this level of prequalification is an exception rather than the norm. Many franchises will clamor for the money of anyone who has a heartbeat.

When aligning capabilities with the franchise model, we employ a (free) tool that can actually predict how a candidate will perform in a hypothetical business environment *before* they invest any money. Based on answers to questions relating to culture, operational preferences, and more, the tool determines which business environments could be the best fit for the individual.

While we don't rely on technology alone to make this critical determination, it is a great starting point to identify activities for which you are best aligned, and those that you're not, and thus carry a higher likelihood of failure.

In addition to assessments, another effective "old school" method is simply to ask the franchisor exactly what the business entails. Unfortunately, most first-time buyers don't know the questions to ask, and each industry has unique variables relating to operations that fall outside the scope of this book.

Possibly the best source for understanding and explaining the day-to-day operations are the franchise owners themselves.

Speaking with existing franchise owners as part of the **validation phase** of your due diligence is great for discovering what a day in the life looks like for an owner.

Again, for the sake of your investment, now is the time to put your ego aside. Speak with the top franchisees, *as well as some that are struggling.* Both of these experiences are very real to the franchisees, and you won't find very many established franchises that do not have at least a few unhappy struggling people in the system.

The important question is with which of these people do you most identify? The struggling franchisees who are full of complaints, or the successful ones? Which of the backgrounds do you most closely match? Are the successful franchise owners from sales backgrounds while you are an engineer? Remember that there is no objective answer to whether a franchise is good or bad, there are only subjective experiences had by franchisees, based on their personalities and background.

If you speak with multiple franchise owners, and you resonate most with those who are struggling, it might be prudent to reconsider this type of business, or even industry.

As franchise brokers, we often take candidates through the validation stage and discussions with franchise owners. It is amazing how varied the experiences can be within the same franchise system. After speaking with multiple owners, the prospective buyer's feedback can range from, "Everyone in the system is unhappy" to "This sounds great I want to move ahead" *even when they spoke with the same franchisees!*

Is a Lamborghini a good or a bad car? It depends on who you ask, and their objectives. If your needs are to transport a family of six around town, and you bought a Lambo, that was a poor choice. You would have been better off with an SUV. It's the same with franchises. You need to match your skills, goals, and objectives with the right franchise.

Overestimation of the buyer's capabilities and the motivation required to perform the work is another major cause of failure. We all like to think we are better, smarter, and more motivated than everyone else, but in a world with 3,500 franchise options, there is no need to pair yourself with a business that is not well aligned with you. Understand the business model entirely, identify the personality types that do best, and then be completely honest about your capabilities. Being unrealistic can be costly.

To further prove that no single franchise is best for everyone, you need only to explore the "About Us" page on the Franchise City website. You will see many of us are, or have been, franchise owners ourselves.

Joe F. was a multi-unit owner of Subway in Canada, which he sold successfully to start his franchise consulting business. Jeff runs a successful Goddard School in Ohio and has done so for more than 13 years. Gary in North Carolina owned a PuroSlean franchise. Pam owns a CG3 Fundraising Franchise in Atlanta.

As you peruse the bios, it becomes apparent that not one of us owns the same franchise!

This observation provides critical insight that can help buyers make better decisions.

The reality is that there is no such thing as a "best" franchise for every buyer. That fact can be validated by our individual franchise-investing choices.

Each one of us has decades of business experience and access to the most detailed information on every available franchise. If there were a single "best" franchise in existence, we would all own it!

But the best franchise for Joe in Saskatchewan, Canada with a CPA background, is not the same for Gary in North Carolina with extensive business development experience. All of us live in different cities, have different exit strategies, and have varying levels of time we can dedicate to operations.

And like all of us, every single investor has a distinctive profile that will include variables unique to themselves that must be considered in order to make a quality investing decision.

Unfortunately, the vast majority of buyers do not start by considering their unique situation. They do not take into account the most important factors, such as long-term goals, exit strategy, operational preferences and market demand.

Instead, they look at the top lists, the books, and the media for a "good" franchise. We saw in previous chapters why that is a terrible idea.

Your city may not need another FroYo franchise. Or maybe it does.

You might be frustrated by the relentless attrition of minimum-wage employees, or you may not.

You might hate B2B selling, or you may love it. Operational requirements need to be examined closely before making a decision.

CHAPTER EIGHT

HOW MUCH MONEY DO FRANCHISES ACTUALLY MAKE?

In addition to the coercive tactics used in the franchising world, another major factor leading to investors making poor decisions is the lack of publicly available financial data.

In an ideal world, franchisors would be legally obliged to post numbers, both gross and net, on a publicly accessible platform so prospective buyers could compare multiple brands and ultimately make a better decision. Today, most buyers speak with one, maybe two franchises, often within the same industry, never knowing if more profitable options exist, inside or outside of the industry.

Within the confines of the franchisor-controlled process, prospective buyers must jump through a number of hoops before receiving any usable information. Many franchises require a complete application, a credit check, and multiple interviews before granting the buyer the "privilege" of seeing the company's financials. And that is if they have them at all. Not all do. It would take months or even years to engage with a sufficient number of franchises to determine which industries, and subsequently which franchises, might be the optimal choice.

By holding the information back, franchisors control the process. They hold the psychological upper hand. They make you jump through hoops to get the information. If it exists at all.

Even when it does, the absence of available data and lack of context allows very low revenue-producing franchises to continue to sell.

Incredibly, franchisors today are not required to disclose any financials at all! In fact, an estimated 50% of franchises do not include any data at all in their Item 19.

Of the franchises that do list earnings, most will list them in a way that presents the brand in a positive light. And the way they do that is arbitrary. There is no standardized template that obliges franchisors to list their data in a meaningful way. They can list a single high-producing franchise, the top 25% on the west coast, or any data they choose.

Ideally, companies will list quartiles, broken down further by regions. This is the gold standard, which, unfortunately, is embraced by the minority of franchises, as the transparency quickly reveals low-performing businesses.

Reputable franchises with nothing to hide will be extremely transparent with their earnings and provide as much data as possible to help buyers understand the financial potential. They will list top and bottom-performing stores along with the average and median revenue of all stores.

The problem is that inexperienced prospective buyers simply don't know this to be the case, and what to look for. If they engage with a franchise and see no Item 19 earnings data, they don't understand that it could be a red flag. If they see a single franchise that indicates a huge gross revenue, they will often extrapolate that these numbers will apply to them.

And even if a comprehensive earnings statement is included, how does a buyer know how those numbers stand up against other industries? They don't.

It is this very scenario that allows so many poorly performing franchises to continue selling to the public.

But how do poorly performing franchises get around providing numbers to prospective franchisees? Again, most buyers don't know any better and assume that all franchise disclosures omit earnings details.

When pressed, less ethical franchisors will fall back on the FTC ruling that prohibits franchisors, or their representatives, from making any earnings claims outside of the information found in Item 19. They will use the law to deflect from the fact they have no verifiable earnings. But the law doesn't prohibit them from including the information at all.

In some cases, they will just let a third party representative (like Harold) make false earnings claims.

Another tactic is to direct the prospective buyer to speak with a very limited number of hand-picked owners who are doing quite well. Most buyers are satisfied when they hear of one or two profitable locations. But if there are 200 franchise locations, and only two are doing well, that is no reason for a celebration.

Franchises will often direct you to speak with their top-performing franchisees, and prospective buyers don't know what to ask in order to determine if this experience is representative of the entire system.

We'll cover that later.

It would be relatively easy for the government to mandate that all franchisors make their earnings available to qualified candidates in a readily accessible location. The reality is that if this happened tomorrow, most of the franchising industry would come to a screeching halt as educated buyers would avoid underperforming franchises and engage only with top brands, of which there are relatively few.

There are, of course, other considerations than just potential earnings. The buyer's operational preferences, market demand, and local demographics should all play a part in the ultimate decision. However, some franchises have such poor overall performance that they should be avoided at all costs, regardless of the suitability to the buyer.

Exploring every available franchise is beyond the scope of any book, but as a general guide we will explore five of the big names in food franchising, and then compare these earnings with other popular industries such as beauty, cleaning, senior care staffing, and others.

We'll also reveal two franchises that generate as much or more as some of the big-name food franchises, for an investment that is much less.

Food Franchises

Many buyers start off thinking they want to own a food franchise. Food franchises are the most visible in our cities, and the ones to which we have had the most exposure. Because of the market prevalence, many buyers assume food franchises are the biggest moneymakers.

But according to a Franchise Business Review report, 51.5% of food franchises earn profits of less than $50,000 a year, and only about 7% of food franchises have profits over $250,000.

The average profit for all restaurants in the report was $82,033.

Not exactly the realm of millionaires. And when you consider that number is the *average*, with many franchisees falling far below that level of revenue, you can see how the investment, time, risk, and potential headaches may not be worth it. Especially when you consider that franchises which cost more than a million dollars to open were included on this list.

In reality, only a very small number of food franchises have stellar profits, and many owners are either struggling financially or have simply bought themselves a job. Also keep in mind that if you are looking at a highly established well-known franchise, *you will receive leftovers in terms of territory*. In the majority of situations, the owners making the most money are in locations that opened up long ago and received the best territories.

An argument we often hear is that someone knows someone who owns 10 Dunkin' Donuts, and they did very well financially. Therefore, as the story goes, any other buyer will also do well with the same investment strategy.

Admittedly many franchisees have done very well with food, but they likely bought their franchise many years ago. Several years' worth of competition has been added to the market since that time, both from other franchises as well as the same franchise stores located nearby. Today's environment is not the environment of yesterday, and competition in the food industry these days is much more intense. And while it is still possible to build a multi-unit empire in food, it is not as easy as it once was.

Let's look at some numbers.

The single highest-grossing food franchise as noted on the QSR50 is Chick-fil-A. An average Chick-fil-A generates $4,160,000 annually, and your investment is only $10,000.

However, despite the impressive revenues, Chick-fil-A has a very different franchise model than most others, and owners do not receive a traditional revenue split, or even ownership of the store.

You'll earn six figures, have limited risk, and be part of an organization with which you might share their traditional values, but you do not own the store or gain any equity. It is also challenging to get a restaurant as Chick-fil-A receives tens of thousands of applications every year and typically only opens 80–100 restaurants. Some owners had waited decades before they were invited to open a store.

Buying a McDonald's will cost $1,263,000 to $2,235,000, not including your real estate. Many people think these numbers include real estate. They do not. McDonald's also has a business model that is unique in that McDonald's corporate purchases the real estate for your location and leases it to you at an agreed-upon rate. It has been suggested that McDonald's is not really in the food business at all. It is actually in the real estate business.

The single highest-earning franchise in the McDonald's system (that was open for at least one year) grossed $12,457,000, and the lowest-earning location generated $557,000. The average systemwide gross revenue for stores open for more than one year is $2,815,000.

Big money! But how much of that does the owner get to keep?

Bear in mind your expenses – employee wages, rent, insurance, royalties and food costs all add up. Also, your location has a huge impact on potential profits as rents in certain cities are very high, as are staffing costs in some states. The ideal scenario is to be in a high-traffic area with low rents and a small payroll, but it can be hard to find premium territories. And while some McDonald's franchises can net hundreds of thousands of dollars, some can, and do, lose money. While specific figures are hard to come by, some sources have suggested that a reasonable net expectation for an "average" single McDonald's is around $150–$200,000 per year. McDonald's has historically been at the higher end of the food industry for net margins, with some suggesting owners have a 20% margin. In this scenario, an average store might net up to $500,000 annually. While this could be the average, local rent, employee costs in your area, location, and dozens of other factors can significantly increase or reduce this number.

Opening a Burger King restaurant will range between $1,877,600 and $3,283,600. Mean average revenue of traditional locations for franchisee-owned stores open at least 12 months was $1,417,443. (Note the average gross revenue is about half that of a McDonald's location.). Burger King's highest-grossing store systemwide in the United States was $4,317,979, which is about one third of McDonald's highest-grossing store. Again, your rent costs, local expenses, and other factors will greatly impact your net, but a 6% net revenue figure seems to be a reasonable average, putting an average Burger King franchise profit at about $85,000 per year. Again, some locations lose money, and some earn far in excess of this number.

Dunkin' Donuts provide detailed insight into their financials, and kudos to them for data that break down earnings throughout the country. At the high end of the chart, if you have a freestanding drive-thru in the north east, you'll average $1,397,936. At the low end, a freestanding restaurant with no drive-thru in the west generates only $974,874. Your cost to open a Dunkin' Donuts will be $465,725 to $1,597,200. The Dunkin' brand's average net revenues are suggested to be around 8-12%. We'll use a 10% average, so if your store is grossing $1 million a year, you can expect an annual profit of approximately $100,000.

The last food franchise we will look at is Subway. Subway has a much lower investment than the other mega brands and, as such, lures many first-time inexperienced investors who make the decision based on the strength of the brand name alone. The average cost to open a traditional Subway location is only $233,325.

Unlike the other franchises listed in this chapter, Subway does not indicate earnings in its disclosure documents. But we can obtain data from the QSR50 and see that an average Subway location grosses $416,000, which is approximately ten times less than an average Chick-fil-A. Subway is the second-lowest earning franchise on the entire QSR50 chart, with only Baskin-Robbins lower at $360,000, at the time of writing.

But remember how Baskin-Robbins was listed as the #13 best franchise overall on the Franchise 500® list? How many buyers used that as validation when they begin their exploration? And how many invested not knowing they were literally buying the lowest-earning food franchise of all major food brands?

Sluggish unit revenues are probably a major reason why Subway closed another 866 stores last year. Even with a 10% margin estimate, an average Subway store would only be netting about $41,000 a year. Again, some locations lose money and some make a lot more, but this is an average. In many locations, you will see an owner-operator behind the counter because often the margins do not allow for a single-store operator to run the business in a semi-passive capacity.

In franchise systems with lower single unit earnings, multi-unit owners can still do well financially, but a single unit, unless it has a great location, is typically not generating significant revenue.

In certain cases, investing in an emerging food franchise as opposed to a highly established brand can provide higher margins and better territory choices. Additionally, master franchise licenses and area developer arrangements are still available, where investors can share profits and franchise fees of multiple franchises within their own territory. Most mega brands sold off their master franchise rights long ago. We'll look at master franchising later.

But how does the food franchise industry compare with other popular sectors such as cleaning, senior care, or staffing? Let's take a look.

Hair Salons, Barbershops and Beauty Franchises

As in our Subway example, these types of franchises often don't generate significant revenue with a single unit. Unlike Subway, however, the operational model is usually conducive to semi-absentee or passive operations. Many owners who choose salons will start their business while still working, open several locations, and generate sufficient capital to quit their jobs.

In our example, we use data from one of the biggest salon brands in the industry. Its Item 19 information includes locations that have been open a minimum of two years. Buyers take note that these locations have taken two years to get to this point. As we mentioned in a previous chapter, franchisors have the autonomy to list any numbers they would like. In this case, they have chosen to include franchises open two or more years. The question you need to ask, as a buyer, is how low were the numbers in years one and two? Remember, the franchisor can't answer this, but existing franchisees should be able to give you their experiences. Most franchise companies suggest buyers only need three months' working capital, yet some locations take 12 months to make a profit. You need to be realistic with yourself. Regardless of what the franchise company tells you about turning a profit after the first quarter, do you have enough working capital to support the business for at least a year?

The gross revenues included in this brand's FDD averaged $371,612, and expenses were $293,870, leaving a yearly operating cash flow average of $77,742. Note the number included is *cash flow*, not net income. Net cash flow can also include the owner's salary, while "net profit" is profit to the company after all expenses are accounted for, including the owner benefit.

In this case, the franchisor has chosen to list cash flow as it shows the business in a more positive light than it would if indicating just net or gross profits. Gross revenue of $371,612 is just a bit higher than the lowest-earning food franchise on the QSR50, so it's not that impressive, but expenses are also likely to be lower than food franchises due to having no tangible product.

Several emerging beauty and niche concepts have higher average earnings that focus on higher-ticket services. Keep in mind that most owners who purchase salons are often looking for a semi-absentee or passive ownership situation. These buyers usually keep their jobs while starting their first salon and ramp up to multiple units. In fact, the average number of salons owned by franchisees after five years in this particular system is six and a half units. As you won't make much with a single location, multi-unit ownership is the preferred option.

The problem we often experience with these highly established franchises is territory availability. Because these mega brands have thousands of units, it can be challenging to find a territory with sufficient room for expansion and not a lot of competition nearby.

Another (free) service we provide is helping buyers determine what brands are available, have open contiguous territory, and make the most sense demographically for their region.

Several emerging salon franchises offer distinctive experiences, such as serving beer and scotch to customers, and several brands have a membership haircutting model, which could prove to be a game changer in the industry. A membership model also helps owners benefit from a more predictable revenue stream.

Your investment to start a single salon will range from around $150,000 at the low end to $500,000+ at the high end. Most brands look for minimal liquidity of $100,000 to $300,000, and net worth between $200,000 and $1 million. Minimum requirements are at the higher end in states such as New York or California which have high rents.

Because of the tight margins, it is essential to determine if the model is even viable in regions with high-leasing costs. We have seen franchises avoid certain markets altogether as it is simply impossible to turn a profit when rents are so high.

Childhood Education Franchises

These include franchises such as Sylvan and Kumon.

Childhood education is typically one of the last sacrifices made in recessionary times, and this industry can be particularly resilient against economic turbulence. Owners will usually manage a location, or teams of mobile tutors, and be actively involved in the oversight of the business.

As with most franchises, companies aren't necessarily looking for franchisees with an educational background, although it helps. More often, they are looking for someone who will network proactively in the community, develop relationships, and grow the business.

The childhood education industry's highest-earning franchise grosses an average of $501,000 annually, which is, incidentally, 53% higher than its closest competitor. Again, as with salons, many owners choose to venture into multi-unit ownership.

These numbers can be deceptive as the size of your location's footprint will have a considerable impact on your bottom line. Some franchises have bigger footprints than others, and some require no physical location at all. Additionally, expenses in your region, such as employee salaries and rent will ultimately dictate how much you can make.

Cleaning Franchises

The single highest-grossing franchise in the cleaning space generates $1,300,000 per year, with the top third of its franchisees making $1,900,000.

This model is not to be confused with buying cleaning contracts, which is a completely different business model with a much smaller investment, typically between $1,000 to $10,000.

The investment for a cleaning franchise ranges from $80,000 to $200,000, which includes your working capital for a period of three to 12 months.

Cleaning can be a lucrative industry, and owners in this model are not wielding the mop themselves (unless an employee doesn't show up). Owners are hiring and managing teams of cleaners, and building the business by networking in their region. Cleaning franchises do not look for candidates with cleaning experience, instead opting for those with business development, managerial or executive backgrounds.

Cleaning franchises will typically focus on residential or commercial clients, or both. Either area carries advantages and disadvantages as determined by the buyer's operational preferences, business goals, and the local economy. The numbers we have referenced in this book are from the residential side of the industry. Earnings vary widely in the cleaning industry with the top brands boasting average gross annual revenues of more than $1 million.

Traditional cleaning franchises should not be confused with "master" cleaning franchising, which is more about selling franchise contracts than actual cleaning.

A master cleaning franchise can be a profitable business for people with a background in sales, or those who have come from executive environments. It is a white-collar role with a blue-collar business. A master cleaning franchise's function is twofold: first to acquire the commercial cleaning contracts in their region, then once the contracts are in place, to sell those contracts via a franchise opportunity to aspiring entrepreneurs who are looking to generate additional income.

The average gross revenue for a cleaning master franchise is $2,800,000, with top earners at $5,800,000. The master franchise has an investment range between $240,000 and $400,000.

Senior Care Franchises

Senior care has seen massive growth, with 10,000 baby boomers turning 65 every day – a trend that will continue for many years. Most seniors prefer to "age at home" and while they don't yet need the care of a facility, they may need some help around the house.

Most senior care franchises provide in-home care to seniors. Similar to the cleaning industry, owners are not expected to have previous industry experience in care, nor will they be providing the care themselves. Instead, franchise companies have a preference for candidates with experience in executive, managerial and business ownership roles, as owners hire and manage teams of caregivers. Not all franchises in this sector earn millions, but some do – up to $1,500,000 on average. So you can, potentially, generate the same revenue as a Taco Bell franchise – $1,600,000 a year – with a much lower investment. A Taco Bell franchise investment will cost an average $1,600,000 to open, while a senior care franchise is around $100,000 to $150,000.

We also have a single senior care company in our franchise portfolio with a unit that generates more than $30,000,000 annually! That figure is almost three times higher than the highest-earning McDonald's location, which calls for a $2,600,000 investment.

Employment and Staffing Franchises

Gross revenues for a popular franchise in the staffing sector sees average mature offices generating almost $6,500,000 annually, and we have seen single locations making over $20,000,000!

The investment for a staffing franchise is around $150,000, which is many times lower than most major food franchises.

Staffing is a very sales-centric model, and prospective owners will want to ensure their own skills and operational preferences match closely with this.

Yes, some owners are making millions. Others who overestimated their abilities have failed.

Which brings us to the million-dollar question: *why doesn't everybody just buy the top-grossing senior care or staffing franchises?* After all, this investment is multiple times lower than fast-food mega brands, with similar – or higher – potential million-dollar earnings.

This is a valid question, and there are several answers.

Firstly, most prospective buyers simply don't know how much franchises make. It would take a lifetime to call all 3,500 franchises, complete their applications, wait for the FDD, and compile the data to determine the highest-earning brands.

Smart investors call us at Franchise City because we have all the data on file!

But more importantly, not everyone has the skills or background to operate a senior care or staffing franchise successfully. If you are a poor fit, you won't be successful, even with the top franchises. Think about it. A Taco Bell will have customers walking in and buying a taco, so it doesn't really matter if you have zero business skills, low motivation or you are not a strong communicator.

But with most senior care, staffing, and service-based businesses, the owner is driving that business forward and needs to have specific skills and ongoing personal motivation to succeed. This alignment is so important that we provide a detailed skills assessment to every candidate with whom we work.

Also keep in mind that gross revenues are not the end of the story. Specific industry margins and operational costs vary widely, and the net profit, or discretionary income, is the number you really want to know.

Unfortunately, as most franchises track their royalties based on gross revenue, few include the net profit in their FDD. Also, due to variances relating to costs specific to your location, your profits in Los Angeles may be lower than someone else's in Idaho. This is why validation is so important. We can determine what an average net profit might be, based on a wide variety of owner capabilities and locations, as well as other data.

Considering the broad range of earnings, it's easy to see why many franchises prefer that you don't know their numbers. When you compare low-revenue brands against highly profitable options, they simply don't hold up. This secrecy is a major reason why so many people end up buying a job or making sub-par decisions. There are very few franchises that have the highest earnings in their respective industries, and the vast majority are mediocre.

While it's important to know the gross earnings in these industries, it is just a starting point. Until you have all the data relevant to how that translates into your own local economy, it is impossible to determine which franchise will be the optimal choice.

The key to success is finding the most profitable franchise, which is best suited to your skills, demographics, market demand, and other relevant criteria.

CHAPTER NINE

TOP EIGHT MISTAKES WHEN BUYING A FRANCHISE

There are many mistakes you can make when buying a franchise, with each vertical market having its own unique set of potential landmines. The subject matter is too varied and vast to cover in a single book, so we will explore some of the most common mistakes.

#1 Buying A Franchise Name, Not the Operational Model

The vast majority of franchise buyers choose a franchise simply because they were attracted to it as a *consumer*. It hits them where their heart is – good sandwiches, a great haircut, a trendy new franchise idea.

A typical scenario goes something like this: a husband and wife are driving along the interstate and stop at a coffee shop that happens to be both quaint and busy. Over coffee, one turns to the other and says, *"This brand would do great in our town."* Fueled with a caffeine hit, their spouse agrees and before they've got home, they've made a call to the franchisor. Several brochures, hype and hoopla-filled phone calls later, they invest $300,000 and now have a store in their city. Hopefully, it works out. Unfortunately, very often, it doesn't.

There is also the *"I love pets! I would make a great pet franchise owner"* rationale that often results in the owner ultimately dreading working in their business and often, eventually closing the doors.

Buyers have no idea that there is far more to these businesses than shampooing Fidos or playing with kittens all day. They had to perform *SALES?*

A readily understood analogy: a cook does not buy a McDonald's franchise.

Just because you understand how to make a hamburger that doesn't mean you should own a restaurant. And while your experience, interests, and skills do come into consideration, they should be matched with the *operational model*, not with what the business sells.

By exploring and understanding the franchise's core operational model, buyers can align their unique skills, strengths, and weaknesses with the business. The actual product or service becomes secondary to the functions you are expected to perform, and in which you should be proficient.

Not many people wake up and say, "I want to own a cleaning franchise", as it conjures up visions of mopping and scrubbing. And frankly, cleaning is not perceived as a glamorous profession.

But the truth is that most cleaning franchises' operational models are executively oriented, meaning it is all about sales, marketing, hiring, managing, landing contracts and closing deals. The fact that cleaning happens to be the service offered is inconsequential. It could be painting, driveway sealing, furniture repair, or anything else with a similar operational model.

And as dull as cleaning and painting might be – they are historically very solid moneymakers, provided of course, the owner is well aligned to the business.

While initial attraction to a franchise may be emotionally driven, be certain you also develop a solid understanding of the operational requirements and day-to-day functions before you sign on the dotted line. Performing activities you dislike or which you are not adept can result in failure.

#2 One Brand Fixation / Emotions over Logic

Our brains are hardwired to fixate. They are also hardwired to manifest highly inaccurate future scenarios based on our own bias.

Once we begin traveling down the path of a specific business, usually one with somewhat romantic underpinnings (yogurt or coffee shop, small restaurant), we desperately want that fantasy to be real.

The considerable desire buyers have for this perfect new life of riches and freedom will often equate directly to the intensity in which any conflicting ideas are pushed aside.

I have personally worked with dozens, perhaps hundreds, of people smitten by a one-brand fixation. It is quite surreal to see people ordinarily possessed of sound minds, arguably above-average intelligence (engineers, accountants, CEOs) who become completely irrational based on a single vision supported by emotion, not logic.

This single-mindedness becomes most prevalent when investors have created a perfect (yet erroneous) mental image of themselves operating the franchise.

Sun shining through gleaming windows as smiling customers rave over yogurt smoothies or cinnamon lattes, and the cash register rings its unending approval.

It's a nice dream but not a foundation on which to bet $300,000.

And once the fantasy is there, it's hard to bring people back to reality. Buyers will block out any negatives that point to the contrary, as they are no longer seeking truth but only reinforcement of their existing belief.

When we work with candidates, we reveal an assortment of metrics that help illustrate the health of a brand and the soundness of a decision. We explore failure rates, potential earnings, franchisee satisfaction, and much more.

Yet, despite presenting comparatively low earnings, dismal success rates, poor long-term industry outlook, heightened risk, and other considerations that would make a rational mind consider changing course, a fixated mind will hear nothing of it.

Sadly, far too often we see people invest $300,000 based on their romantic notion, and six to 12 months later, list their "life dream" on BizBuySell for $75,000. Take a look! There are hundreds of fire sales begging for whatever the owners can recoup because their utopian fantasy became a financial nightmare. Ironically, the next person in line with the $75,000 often has the same notion. And the industry churns onward simply because of the irrational optimism of franchise buyers.

Remember the beginning of the book when we noted the shocking number of franchise failures? Single-brand fixation is another culprit that contributes to those numbers.

The truth is there is not a single franchise of the 3,500+ that does not have negative attributes of some sort. High attrition, high failure rates, seasonality, poor management, nearing the end of the industry growth curve, being at the beginning of the industry growth curve, junior brand, high royalties, limited support, strong sales requirement – they all have some weaknesses alongside their strengths. But under the right ownership, these weaknesses can be minimized or even become strengths *if the investor has not been oblivious to their existence*.

Despite being the most romanticized franchise type, retail shops are one of the most difficult to turn around if walk-in traffic is absent and your local demand is low. When business is slow, there is just not a lot to be done. With service-based brands, you have a much greater ability to ratchet up sales efforts and increase the bottom line. That is assuming you are willing and able to do so!

But few people want to hear about cleaning or painting when they could have a small, romantic coffee shop. Or a pub or burger joint. "We don't care if the industry has over a 50% failure rate, we will be the exception which makes it work! **I feel it in my bones!**"

The outcome of being guided by gut feelings and sentiment rather than logic and hard facts? See the opening chapter regarding how the majority of franchisees fail.

Once the fixation takes place, and when prospective franchisees engage directly with the franchisor, they are presented with positive information that is biased from the franchisor's point of view. Not to insinuate a franchisor will outright mislead (although as previously noted, there are some less-than-ethical operators), but most will focus on positives while glossing over the negatives. Much like a parent who perceives their own child to be the brightest and best, a franchisor will also very often harbor a biased opinion.

Surprisingly, many prospective franchise buyers stop their research right where it should begin. They accept the franchisors' multiple industry awards, historical earnings and many years in business as proof positive that they will also do well.

They speak with the franchisor with no other goal in mind than to *validate their own fantasies* of a glorious life, making millions.

Many buyers want to drink the Kool-Aid. We deal with dozens of clients every month, and not a week goes by without us being asked to provide a second opinion regarding a franchise of their choice because we haven't painted it in an entirely positive light and have highlighted some potential negatives! People want the perfect dream of business ownership. When we puncture that dream with some reality checks, many prefer to close their minds to us rather than leave the comfort of their delusion, and this often results in their own financial destruction.

The solution is to explore several brands and even industries. Explore their strengths and weaknesses *unemotionally*. Find the brand whose weaknesses (because *all* brands have weaknesses) will not be debilitating to you, and whose strengths are most in alignment. Review them all with a critical mindset, and only when you're satisfied that you have a clear picture should you make an educated decision. Fixating only on the positive aspects of one brand is a terrible way to invest.

Yes, it is advisable and commendable to harbor a positive outlook for your future business, but too many investors allow a perfect vision to propel them forward while putting on blinders to potential negatives.

Stay critical, don't let emotion cloud judgment, and never fixate on a single franchise. Always compare multiple options with a clear and level head.

#3 Buying a Job

As franchise industry professionals, we are privy to the earnings of most available franchises. Some are very high, others low. As crucial as it is to the buying decision, this information is not easy for the general public to come by. It is also one of the last details most franchisors will provide for you, and usually only after several interviews and an application.

Why? Well, as we've covered earlier, in an effort to protect franchise buyers from exaggerated earnings claims, the FTC has disallowed any franchisor or broker from making *any* potential earnings claims outside of what is included in their FDD. This makes for a difficult presentation as generally the first question a prospect asks is "How much can I make?"

While protecting consumers on one level, this gag order has harmed them on another. As it stands, the prospective buyer must first engage the franchisor, become qualified, fill out an application, have several discussions, and only then will they be mailed the FDD.

Within the FDD, the franchisor might legally disclose their earnings in the previously discussed Item 19 of the document. Or they might not. It is not mandatory.

Most franchise shoppers have neither the time nor the inclination to research dozens of franchises, and if they do, their selections are often within the same vertical market and investment level. As such, they often reflect similar earnings. Many never look beyond a single brand.

Many aspiring entrepreneurs buy a low-grossing franchise for $100,000+, spend hard days working on growing the business only to max out at $40-60,000 a year in cash flow, or even less. They have bought a job.

It is also astounding how few buyers will bother to educate themselves on financial basics prior to investing hundreds of thousands of dollars. Many don't understand the concepts of "net profit", "earnings before interest, taxes, depreciation and amortization", which you might see written as "EBITDA", or "discretionary earnings".

EBITDA figures allow the buyer to exclude non-operating expenses from the financials. These expenses include debt financing, depreciation, capital structure and taxes. EBITDA is essentially company earnings with loan interest, depreciation, amortization and taxes added back.

Some franchises provide net income, some provide cash flow and discretionary earnings, some provide gross revenue. Some provide nothing at all.

Discretionary income and net profit are different. Discretionary income includes monies that have been included in the owner benefit. For example, if your business generates $80,000 in discretionary earnings, but you paid yourself a salary of $80,000, the *net profit* for your business would be zero!

In businesses where the owner intends to draw a salary rather than rely on the net earning power of the business alone, discretionary earnings are a reliable indicator of how much benefit the business will be providing.

Also included in the discretionary earnings, or "owner cash flow" are owner perks and non-recurring expenses, such as company vehicle payments, business-related meals and entertainment, even the owner's health insurance.

Once these expenses, which can be substantial, have been covered, is there enough net profit remaining for the business? Also, remember that the business, if incorporated, and the owner will become two distinct entities.

#4 A $500,000 Ego

Everyone wants to be the smartest and the best at everything they do. It is a natural human condition. We often feel we know more than everyone else. But when it comes to investigating franchises, our own ego can be costly .

Along with our ego is the natural human need for safety. We all want to protect ourselves from negative outside influence. We are especially wary of any "advice". In a post-Madoff world (for those living under a rock, Bernie Madoff facilitated a Ponzi scheme in which investors were promised sensational returns on their investments – the money ended up in his bank account, and he ended up in jail), this mistrust of other people's suggestions ranges from the waitress promoting the special of the day to the realtor suggesting a "hot" location. We are a mistrustful bunch.

In certain cases, this attitude is justified. But if ego and fear impair your ability to analyze and evaluate data effectively, or even ignore key points, it needs to be addressed. Investors driven by emotion don't make good buying decisions. Educated, cautious, well-researched investors who avoid hype will often make great ones.

Several years ago, an investor came to us inquiring about a popular sandwich franchise resale in a nearby city location. We took a quick look and within five minutes, provided him with multiple reasons why this might be a bad investment. We suggested several alternatives to which the investor completely closed their mind.

In the end, after encountering a brick wall, we suggested that instead of the full-asking price, he offered half that, as it was likely that the desperate seller would jump at any offer.

Driven by his emotional bias, and entirely convinced of his own infallibility and business prowess, the investor ignored our advice, believing we were misinformed at best or misleading at worst. This was a very well-known franchise brand after all, with thousands of locations. It was included in all the top lists and mentioned favorably throughout the media. The buyer had succumbed to the very tactics we noted in the first part of the book.

A mere five days later, after falling for manipulative "sense of urgency" tactics on the sellers' part, the investor offered the full asking price. Sigh.

Eighteen months later, we heard the investor had placed all his savings into keeping this store afloat but ultimately had to close the doors. It is heartbreaking to see people go through this. Had he kept an open mind and tethered his ego, he may have purchased a franchise that would have provided a great retirement. And the sad thing is this is not an isolated incident. The exact same scenario happens with predictable regularity.

Maintaining an open mind and reining in the ego throughout the due diligence process is critical. An ego-driven fixation on any brand prior to extensive research can be costly – even if it appears to be "the deal of the century".

Are you willing to gamble hundreds of thousands of dollars on the assumption you know something that others don't?

#5 Inappropriate Financing

Nobody goes into franchising expecting to fail. Armed with the best intentions, most aspiring entrepreneurs put little thought into contingency or failure planning. In the event of failure, inappropriate financing can create a "double whammy".

Once the franchise has been selected, most people are justifiably eager to start their business. This often lends itself to engaging the most expedient methods to access readily available cash. The first choice of many is to borrow from the equity in their home, otherwise known as a home equity line of credit or HELOC.

In the event the business thrives, this is not such a terrible thing. But can you imagine your business closing after all that hard work, and then losing your home as well?

Franchise investors should step back and examine their risk tolerance realistically.

As a society, we have conditioned ourselves to leverage the maximum amount possible without blinking an eye. But statistics tell us that investing higher amounts in the hopes of greater gains is not a sound strategy. In fact there are many franchises under $100,000 investment that can be extremely profitable. Additionally, when we take historical franchise failure rates into consideration, high investment amounts don't necessarily reflect higher probabilities of success or higher earnings.

Once buyers determine a realistic investment budget, the next step is to choose appropriate financing. The strategy should be suited to your specific situation.

Beyond traditional financing choices, other options are available, some of which carry significant tax benefits. For example, in the USA a well-planned 401k rollover or ROBS (rollover as business startups) can have you withdrawing monies tax-free (up to a 40% tax savings) from a low-yielding portfolio and re-directing funds into your own business. You can potentially also draw a salary, which can provide a significant reduction in stress, particularly in the initial stages of opening the business.

#6 Assuming a Franchise is Less Work

Part of the appeal of franchise ownership is leveraging an established system and operational model.

Many of the more challenging business elements and processes, such as logos and branding, product sourcing, customer acquisition, marketing and sales, have been streamlined and refined, making a franchisee's job much easier.

Unfortunately, many buyers misinterpret these benefits as making it "easy" to own a franchise. This is far from the truth.

Each franchise has unique operational requirements that an individual franchise owner must fulfill. Despite having many of the daily tasks listed clearly in the operations manual, the franchisee will have many days, weeks and years of work ahead of them. This is why we recommend aligning oneself with the core operational model rather than the franchise brand. Going to work, regardless of how much money you make, is no fun if you don't enjoy doing it or are not particularly good at it.

Like any other business, a franchise will require an investment of time, money and effort. How much you get out will be proportionate to how much you put in. If you choose wisely, have realistic expectations, and understand the franchisor's expectations, you can do quite well.

If you are seeking the "perfect" business where you simply sit back and the money flows in, you might be better served investing in a $29 online "Super Turbo Cash Money Machine". At least you won't lose too much money!

Owning a franchise, like any other business, is hard work, but it can be enjoyable. If you have matched your skills, do your research, and have realistic expectations, franchisees can do extremely well.

#7 Don't Believe the Hype

Like many industries, franchising has created a system of awards and accolades relating to allegedly outstanding achievements among its ranks.

New award groups such as "Fastest-Growing Potato-Based Franchise" (yes we made that one up) are constantly being created. As meaningless as these awards are, many prospective buyers accept them as validation that a franchise is successful.

Consider the "fastest-growth" franchise award. Simply because a franchise has sold many outlets does not imply anything other than what it states. In fact, a "hard-selling" franchise may also be one with lousy franchisee support. Some of the slow-moving franchise brands move slow by choice and decide to focus on outstanding franchisee support rather than amassing huge swaths of territory.

Similarly, just because a brand sells a bazillion sandwiches a year, or has great prices, or the best tasting fries, it has little relation to how happy or how successful you will be as an owner. In fact, most existing food-service franchisees complain about being obliged to provide those discount sandwiches because the margins are so low!

Certain awards might indicate some levels of credibility, success, and industry acceptance. Those successes may not directly benefit you as a prospective franchisee. Don't be propelled forward by awards, and certainly don't use them as a foundational cornerstone on which to rationalize your decisions.

We regularly work with clients looking at popular brands, and when we present statistics and facts trending towards the negative, their counter-argument more often than not is: "But they are a top fastest-growing franchise" or some other such award.

If one of the reasons for choosing your franchise is an industry award, you may want to dig deeper for more compelling facts. Be sure to make decisions based on sound business analysis and personal suitability rather than the franchise flavor of the month.

#8 Misinterpreting the Numbers

Investors that take the time to research and compare several franchise brands should be commended. Many buyers seldom look at more than one.

When making a selection from say four brands in the same vertical market, many prospective franchisees base their selection on a single factor, which is the lowest initial investment.

Franchises in the same vertical market will have different operational strategies, efficiencies, inventory purchase minimums, and product markups. For example, if you buy XYZ concrete refinishing franchise for $39,000, but you are obliged to buy their coatings for $5 a square foot, and you turn down ABC franchise for $69,000 despite their coatings being provided for a dollar and a half a square foot, you have likely made a poor decision.

With XYZ franchise, you may have initially saved yourself $30,000, but you will be less competitive in the market. ABC franchise charges more at the front end, and has chosen to monetize the initial franchise fee rather than tie a ball and chain to its franchisees. ABC franchise is probably a far better deal, and the franchisee would have recouped that $30,000 difference in a few months of operations. XYZ franchise will be forever operating at a market disadvantage, having to quote higher just to maintain reasonable margins.

Ever bought an inkjet printer? You buy the printer for $30, then find out the replacement ink cartridges cost more than the printer itself. In retrospect, and depending on your printing needs, you may have been better off paying more upfront for a laser printer. Franchising, and your initial investment, should be considered much in the same way, particularly if you are obliged to purchase goods directly from corporate.

This example is an oversimplification of the subject, but it does illustrate the importance of understanding the business expense and revenue model, and your specific obligations to purchase supplies from the franchisor. If you are bound to purchase supplies at inflated costs, it won't make much difference how much business you get. In the past (and present), fast-food franchises have been sued by franchisees over perceived unfair practices concerning mandatory supplies and inflated markups.

Make sure you understand the operational model, the profit centers and how each franchise stacks up against each other. Investigate royalties, ad spend requirements, product purchase minimums and costs. Item 8 in the FDD outlines products, supplies and inventory, and must also indicate if the franchisor generates a profit from them.

Would you rather invest $69,000 and generate $180,000 a year or spend $30,000 and go under? That choice should be obvious. The lowest-cost franchise is not always the best choice, and there are many financial dynamics that should be considered beyond your initial investment.

CHAPTER TEN

UNDERSTANDING THE FDD

The franchise disclosure document or FDD is a critical component of the due diligence process. By law, franchisors must provide the FDD to all candidates before they sign on the dotted line.

Having standardized disclosure available is another significant benefit of franchising. As a potential buyer, you should take advantage of this by thoroughly understanding the FDD and the expectations placed on you as a new franchisee. Hiring an attorney experienced in franchise law will cost money upfront but can save you money and heartache in the future.

There is a disclosure waiting period from when you sign the FDD to when you can buy the franchise, which is a federally mandated 14 days. So even if you wanted to, you couldn't invest for 14 days after receiving and signing the FDD. There is also a seven-day waiting period between the franchise agreement. However, most franchises will send both the FDD and the franchise agreement at the same time and have the waiting periods run concurrently.

Sadly, some buyers simply gloss over the FDD and agreement (which can amount to 400 pages combined), assuming the good folks at ABC franchising would not steer them wrong. And that may be the case. But there is no shortage of disagreements and lawsuits stemming from investors that felt wronged by the franchisor.

A considerable advantage when reading the FDD is the standardized format. The document is a daunting 200 pages long and it can seem overwhelming, but once you break it down to its constituent parts (there are 23 in total), and you know what to look for, the task of reading and digesting it becomes much more manageable.

For example, Item 19 is always the financial disclosure and Item 5 always covers the franchise fees. The FDD must also include the franchisor's financial well-being, any lawsuits against them, your anticipated costs and operating expenses, as well as the contact numbers of existing owners and people who have left the system over the past year.

Item 8, as we mentioned in the previous chapter, is an often-overlooked section that outlines your responsibility to purchase or lease goods through the franchisor or authorized suppliers. Make sure you understand precisely what you are expected to buy, for how much, and whether there are potential penalties or minimum requirements. Be sure to take the time to research the material costs at current market rates to see if these prices are inflated. If you are obligated contractually to purchase goods at non-competitive rates, this will make the franchisor a lot of money, and make you very unhappy. Legally, the franchisor will have to disclose if they are making a profit from any of the transactions.

So, when the franchisor finally does agree to send you the documents, usually after several phone calls, you may consider the document to be too long and complex to understand, and put it away to look at "tomorrow". Or worse, you may decide to just rely on what the franchisor has told you. Don't.

Understanding an FDD is not that difficult, and it contains some fantastic information that will help you learn a lot.

Ultimately buyers should consider having the FDD and agreement vetted by a competent FRANCHISE lawyer. We stress *franchise* lawyer because a non-specialist attorney, who doesn't have specific experience in these agreements, will often consider it overly restrictive. But a franchise lawyer understands that is the nature of all FDDs and can advise you accordingly, in context of all the other agreements they have seen.

A non-franchise lawyer often won't understand that every franchise is highly regulated, right down to how many pickles your employees put on a burger. An inexperienced lawyer might recommend you keep away as there are too many requirements and restrictions, and they're all in favor of the franchisor. And they wouldn't necessarily be wrong. An experienced franchise attorney understands the context of the documents, the nature of an FDD and can advise accordingly.

Non-specialist lawyers may also miss critical details that a franchise specialist will immediately uncover.

However, before hiring a lawyer, it can be financially prudent to see if you, on your own, can uncover any fine print that might be a "dealbreaker".

Once you have a basic understanding of how to read the FDD, take a look through the document.. You can then determine whether it is worth your time and money to pay a lawyer to look at it. If any points are not to your liking and you choose not to proceed, you just saved money on a lawyer. If you don't see any objectionable content, then it is time to hire your lawyer to dig more deeply into the document.

Don't let the legal jargon scare you. The FDD is created in such a way that it can be jarring, particularly after hearing all the smooth sales talk. It contains cold, hard facts, disclaimers, and disclosures. This is the nature of the document and not necessarily warnings specific to your particular franchise.

Contents of the FDD

The first page of the FDD will be a general overview of the franchise and investment amounts. If you've been working with the franchisor, most of this information will already be known to you.

The Table of Contents page outlines the 23 items of the FDD. This is a standardized format, and every FDD has the same table of contents and the same 23 items.

Item 1. The Franchisor and Any Parents, Predecessors, and Affiliates. This will be a few paragraphs regarding the business, date of incorporation, and whether the franchise is owned or controlled by other entities, where its principal place of business is located, its formal operating name, and further pertinent details. It will also list relevant information regarding the franchise, applicable regulations, and potential competition. This can be helpful as it will provide insight into who your local competition might be. Does your area have a large number of stores operating a similar business to you? If so, make a note.

Item 2. Business Experience. This will outline all the people involved in the franchise. A small tip: Google the names of the people in the FDD. See what comes up. Did they come from other failed franchises? Have they been involved in lawsuits? Check out their LinkedIn profiles. Experienced management of a franchise system is essential, and you should be confident in the franchise system itself, as well as the people running it. While franchisors are obliged to disclose legal problems and bankruptcies involving the principals, less ethical franchises do play fast and loose with the facts. Google is your friend.

Item 3. Litigation. Has the franchise sued anyone, or been sued itself? Keep in mind, it's not the end of the world if you see lawsuits. Franchising is a very litigious industry, and many established franchises will have a lawsuit or two (or more!) in their books, particularly larger franchise systems.

That said, you should closely examine the nature of these lawsuits. If you see several instances of franchisees suing for reasons of fraud, misrepresentation, or breach of contract, you may want to look elsewhere or, at the very minimum, increase your level of due diligence.

Has the franchise sued its own franchisees on multiple occasions? If there is a large number of franchisees being sued, this can also be a red flag. A happy organization with minimal legal issues is typically a profitable organization.

Item 4. Bankruptcy. Has the franchise or any of its principals been declared bankrupt? If so, they will have to list this in the FDD. Take note that any historical bankruptcies by the principals must be disclosed even outside of this organization. If a director in the company made a bad real estate deal and declared bankruptcy, they'll have to list it. Now is that relevant to the operations of this business? That will be your decision.

Item 5. Initial Fees. This is a quick breakdown of what your initial fees will be. Examine these carefully as some of the fees may not have been disclosed during the sales presentation. You will see costs related to training, goods and services, your franchise fee, and others. These will be payable before you open for business.

Item 6. Other Fees. These are the applicable fees beyond your initial fees that are paid to the franchise or other affiliates. These will typically include royalty payments, marketing, promotional expenses, costs for advertising (which may be local and national), training fees, technology fees, software fees, and others.

Buried within these fees will be costs such as the transfer fee – that's how much you will get charged if you sell your franchise – and a renewal fee – that's how much it will cost you if you renew your license after the term expires. This is another piece of information you need to look for – the length of the franchise term. We'll see that listed later in the FDD. Item 6 will also outline late fee charges and if there are any fines for noncompliance. Read this item carefully, as in some FDDs you can be fined thousands of dollars for infractions as small as putting a wrong ingredient in the food! You can also be fined thousands of dollars for losing the operations manuals. And if you don't pay your fine on time, Item 6 will outline how much interest the company is going to charge you.

Item 7. Your estimated total initial investment. This item provides a range from low to high of what your entire investment will be for the franchise, including the franchise fee, training, signage, leasehold improvements, furniture, initial inventory, and working capital.

As a buyer, you can use these numbers to estimate how much your total financial outlay will be in your specific area. If you live in a smaller city, your costs will likely be less than in larger, more expensive cities. Remember, these numbers are not estimates; these are the ranges, from low to high, of how much franchise owners have actually invested to get their franchise started.

At the bottom of the chart is the total range for your estimated costs. Item 7 will also have several paragraphs outlining how the funds are allocated, as well as to whom the funds are payable.

Note that in the total investment, franchisors often include a certain amount allocated to working capital, which is usually three months.

This does not mean you can expect to be cash-flow positive in that time! It can be prudent to have working capital well in excess of this limited time frame.

How can you determine how much you will really need to reach profitability? You can ask the franchisor, but speaking with existing franchisees will help gain a more accurate estimate of the actual time it took to reach profitability and return on investment (ROI).

Contact several owners to understand the range from shortest to longest, and ensure your own capital reserves are sufficient for a worst-case scenario.

Most franchisors have a minimum net worth requirement to ensure franchisees don't have to close the doors if they are still in the red after the three months of operating capital is gone.

Item 8. Restrictions on Sources of Products and Services. An essential item if you are selling food or buying products from the franchisor.

Do you need to buy their proprietary cleaning products? Are you required to buy their hamburger meat? Do you need to use their point of sale systems? Item 8 will also indicate if the franchisor is making a profit, and how much profit is made from them selling goods or services to franchisees.

As noted in the previous chapter, if you are forced to purchase goods or supplies at unrealistically elevated costs, your business may not be competitive, especially in industries that already have razor-thin margins. Always be sure you are not required to buy goods from the franchisor at unrealistic prices.

One of the implied benefits of buying a franchise is the volume buying power, but that is not always the case. Check competition and wholesalers to determine whether the prices you are expected to pay are indeed equitable.

Item 9. Franchisee's Obligations. At first glance, this appears to be a fairly short section. Unfortunately, Item 9 references specific sections in the actual franchise *agreement* (even more pages!) that cover these obligations in greater detail. This item can be a bit time-consuming, switching back and forth between the franchise agreement and the FDD, but it's worth reading as it's important you understand what you are expected to do during the life of the contract.

There are a wide variety of obligations covered, ranging from policies, procedures, customer service requirements, the owner's actual participation requirements, renewal, advertising, and a lot more. Be sure you are comfortable with the obligations before you sign, as being in contravention of any of these could cost you your franchise. If your preference is to have a manager run the business while you play golf, and the agreement requires you to personally be on site, you teeing off every day would be in contravention of the contract and could lose you the franchise. Make sure their expectations are in alignment with your own expectations.

Item 10. Financing. Is there any financing available? Some franchises provide in-house financing, while others rely on third-party providers. You may also want to speak with your broker or franchise consultant as there are several options available, including redirecting your 401k funds to your own business. This can have enormous tax benefits, but there are also set up fees and ongoing costs.

There may also be financing programs specific to your situation, such as veteran or minority funding options.

Item 11. Franchisor's Assistance, Advertising, Computer Systems, and Training. After reading about everything the franchisor is taking, finally, here is what they will do for you! This might include site selection, helping you find a location, providing floor plans, lists of suppliers and vendors, training, operations manuals, advertising collateral, and more.

Make a note of things such as their social media policy and website policies. Do you need to pay for a website? Can you run your own local social media campaigns? If you are personally adept at these functions, you may want a franchise that allows you to have more involvement. Costs of computers and point of sale systems are also included if applicable.

Item 12. Territory. Will you be granted an exclusive territory, and if so, what does it include? How is it defined? Is it decided by population density or a geographic radius? Some franchises, which award based on territory size alone, may hobble franchisees who don't have a sufficient customer base within that radius. For example, if you own a one-square-mile territory in Florida, where the client base is largely seniors, or the same size in Utah, whose population is on average 31 years old, the territory in Florida may not be as fruitful. Similarly, if your franchise provides business services and very few qualified businesses exist within your square mile, you will struggle.

If you do not have a protected or exclusive area, could you be facing competition from fellow franchise owners? Some franchises offer only location protection, meaning anything outside your store is fair game for another franchisor to set up a store. Even right next door!

In some types of businesses having a specific territory can actually be restrictive. Certain consulting franchises, for example, will protect individual accounts, but not the territory. There is no simple answer to whether this is good or bad, and the ramifications are too complex to cover in this book. Just be aware of what the territorial rights are, and compare those with other franchises.

Also, make a note of any provisions requiring you to achieve specific sales levels to retain the territory. If you do not reach the minimums, will you lose the franchise?

Are you able to solicit orders outside your territory? What happens if a prospective customer calls you from just one block outside your region? Can you service that customer, or will you need to refer them to the neighboring franchise owner? Do you receive a fee for doing so?

We suggest candidates compare at least three or four franchises to make sure they identify brands that have the lowest royalties, largest territories, and best support. Not all franchises will have protected or exclusive territories and, depending on the industry, that scenario can actually make sense. Also determine what your options might be for territory expansion if applicable.

If you are concerned about similar stores opening nearby, and your budget will permit, you can always ask the franchisor for a "right of first refusal", meaning it will offer you a future store first before contacting another owner. This is not always possible, particularly with more established franchises, but it never hurts to ask.

Item 13. Trademarks. These are the company's trademarks that will be provided for your use if you buy the franchise. If this is a very new company, the trademarks may not actually be registered. If so, there is a small chance this could potentially cause issues down the line with another company disputing the use of the trademark.

Item 14. Patents, Copyrights, and Proprietary Information. This is legal speak outlining the extent of control over the franchise's proprietary information and your limits of use.

Item 15. Obligation to Participate in the Actual Operations of the Franchise Business. This item is particularly important if you are looking for a passive operation business. Some franchises require actual owner involvement in the day-to-day business. Others allow you to install a designated manager to run your shop. Make sure that whatever you choose, it is in alignment with your business goals.

Remember that even if passive operations are permitted, a passive business becomes "hands on" very quickly if your manager quits or some other emergency takes place that your manager can't handle on their own. Many franchises will downplay the actual time commitment required to run the business, and while in theory it could be run passively, in real life that can prove not to be the case.

Ask other franchise owners how long it took them to become fully passive and how much time did they dedicate to the business for this to work. If a franchisee is not happy, or was sold promises of easy wealth, they'll let you know! It's prudent to also call franchisees who have left the system, as they will typically have the most critical feedback. Not that you only want to listen to gloom and doom, but you should have input that includes both positive and negative.

During validation, keep in mind that you are not assessing the previous franchise owners, you are evaluating the franchise system. Some owners just might not have been a good fit and they failed despite an excellent franchise support structure.

Item 16. Restrictions on What the Franchisee May Sell. This item is quite important and ties back to Item 8. Again, you want to be sure that these restrictions are mutually beneficial, and are not forcing you to sell overpriced single-source goods.

With the purchasing power of a company such as McDonald's, it obviously makes sense to have standardized food sources to lower costs and maintain consistency.

Many cleaning franchises also have proprietary cleaning materials they manufacture. Unscrupulous franchises may just use this as a profit center, selling products at huge margins to contractually obligated franchisees. Always make sure existing franchisees are happy with the arrangement, and undue profit is not gouged from owners.

Item 17. Renewal, Termination, Transfer, and Dispute Resolution. How long is the term? Most franchise agreements range between five and 20 years. How much does it cost to renew? What is considered just cause for termination or non-renewal? What rights are available to you legally? What happens in the case of breach of contract? What happens in the case of death or disability? It is also important to understand non-compete provisions. Can you operate other businesses during the term? If your plan is to keep an existing business or career, is that permissible under the contract terms?

Item 18. Public Figures. Does the franchisor use any public figures or celebrities to promote the franchise? You might think this is unimportant, but in the digital age (and also the age of scandals), you should be aware of any celebrity names associated with the brand. What is this person's reputation? Lifestyle?

Remember Jared Fogle, the spokesperson for Subway? After being sentenced to prison for some rather foul deeds, it would not be inaccurate to suggest that every franchise owner in that system suffered from the negative press he generated. While the bad publicity is not the only reason for Subway's decline, it certainly didn't help.

Item 19. Financial Performance Representations. Item 19 contains the topic most buyers include at the top of their question list – *"How much money can I make with this franchise?"*

As noted, not every franchise lists its financial performance. And not every franchise lists figures in the same way. Franchises have the legal autonomy to use any statistics they wish or not list any numbers at all. Ensure you understand if the data shown is an average of all locations or a smaller cross section of locations.

For example, if a frozen yogurt shop only shows profits from the top 10 stores in Florida, that doesn't provide you with any relevant data for you opening up in Alaska. If the franchisor has not laid out their numbers broken down regionally, you should find out whether some geographic regions are lower producing than others.

Whether the franchise does or doesn't list the numbers, it's always wise to call an assortment of existing franchisees and get a feel of their financial situation, and how long it took them to break even. If franchisees aren't happy about their earnings, they will let you know!

Remember that when you ask the franchise company, or their representatives, how much you could make, they are legally prohibited from providing any other numbers than those listed in the

Item 19. If they have no numbers listed, they cannot make any claims or even imply that you could make a certain amount. There are severe penalties for making illegal earnings claims, but many companies play fast and loose with the rules as we explained in the initial chapters.

While these laws bind the franchise company and any agents that represent them, *franchise owners* are not bound by the same rules. And while not every franchise owner will share their financials with you, many will.

Item 20. List of Outlets and Franchisee Information. This is very important as it will show you information over the past three years of how many franchise units were opened, transferred, or closed.

If you see negative numbers related to store closures, that is a big red flag. Keep in mind that these numbers represent the "net" number of stores closed. So if the franchise sold 20 locations last year and closed 30, the Item 20 section will only indicate net closures of 10.

A quick way to calculate how many stores were closed the previous year is to look in the agreement section. By law, franchises must list all their current franchise owners as well as any who left the system in that year. In some cases, the franchise will identify store transfers versus closures, but not all do.

If the list includes a large number of franchisees who left the system, this can be a red flag. Keep in mind that a smaller emerging franchise might not have any, and most larger franchises will have several. A few closures and/or transfers are to be expected.

Something you also want to watch out for is what is called franchise "churning". Instead of letting unprofitable stores close, the franchisor sells the store to an unsuspecting new owner. That struggling location won't now show up as a net change in the store openings or closures. Where it will show up is lower down in the "transfers" section.

Item 21. Financial Statements. These are the financial statements, not for individual franchisees as seen in the Item 19, but the franchise corporation as a whole. If the company's financials look frail, how will that impact its ability to help you be successful?

Item 22. Contracts. This is an overview of all of the contracts, including the franchise agreement and others such as general release forms, state-specific agreements, development agreements, etc.

And finally, **Item 23. Receipts.** That is the portion you must return to the franchisor to acknowledge receipt of the FDD. You will have a minimum of 14 days from the receipt acknowledgment before you can invest, so if you have time constraints do this as soon as possible. Digital signatures are also permissible, so your franchisor may send you a copy via DocuSign or a similar service.

Beyond the FDD is the actual franchise agreement itself. If you are happy with the FDD, you will now want to have a qualified franchise attorney look everything over.

CHAPTER ELEVEN
MASTER FRANCHISING

As we examine the franchise structure, it becomes apparent that the franchisor has a pretty sweet gig.

It sells the franchise to a buyer and receives a healthy franchise fee, while the buyer assumes all the business risks by leveraging their own money. If the franchise goes under, the franchisor loses nothing. If it does well, the franchisor receives ongoing royalties.

Obviously, the franchisor takes little risk and has strong potential for future rewards.

But there is a way for an independent buyer to enjoy many of the benefits typically afforded only to franchisors. Master franchising.

Master franchising has been used successfully by hundreds of franchises over decades. It helps franchisors expand quickly, and it can help the franchisee, in essence, become a mini-franchisor within a specific region.

There are master franchise options in many industries, including fitness, food, pet care, senior care and cleaning.

Master franchising is an arrangement where the franchise company provides the brand's rights and responsibilities within a given geographic territory. Master franchise rights can be for an entire country or a single city.

Essentially, the master franchisee has purchased the rights to develop that particular franchise brand within their allocated territory.

Master franchising (and similarly, area development rights) are often used for international expansion. For example, if an existing USA-based franchise wishes to enter another country, they could sell the master franchising rights to someone in Canada or anywhere in the world. The master franchisee in that country essentially becomes a franchisor themselves and begins to develop and sell unit franchises within their territory while also supporting the franchisees in their system. As they are local to the region, they naturally have a greater understanding of the local culture, customs, and market demand than a franchisor from outside the area.

The franchisor benefits from an immediate infusion of cash from the sale of the master franchise, and now has someone in the region with an intimate understanding of the local economic, business, demographic and cultural landscapes.

The master franchisee benefits from the brand's strength, franchisor support, established systems and processes, and now sells (or opens) franchises, sharing the ongoing royalties and franchise fees from locations in their territory.

In essence, the master franchisee becomes a mini-franchisor within that territory.

Most revenue splits are 50/50 on both the franchisee fees collected as well as ongoing royalties. In addition to opening their own franchise, the master franchisee can also sell unit franchises within their territory.

Let's look at a typical master scenario. Our master franchisee buys master franchise rights for 10 licenses in Ontario, Canada, for $200,000. Depending on the agreement, they could sell all 10 locations, open and operate five themselves and sell five to other franchisees, or any variation they prefer. Not all master franchise agreements require you to open and operate a franchise yourself; some mean you have purely a development role.

The master franchisee recruits potential franchisees in their area, and once a qualified candidate is recruited, the master assists them in opening their own location. The master provides support and training at a local level.

A master franchisee is of great benefit to the franchisor as they help expand into multiple locations without the franchisor having to increase their internal marketing, sales, or training departments.

The master franchisee benefits with additional cash flow via the sale of franchise units. For example, if the franchise fee is $40,000, the master would receive $20,000 in a 50/50 split scenario. If the master had paid $200,000 for the master franchise rights, they would need to sell all 10 locations to break even. Any royalties or profit generated by their own location would be a bonus.

Suppose a master franchisee has 10 locations operating in their territory and receives 50% of all these locations' royalties. In this scenario, the added royalties become a solid income stream that becomes mostly passive after all the locations are operational.

Every franchisor has varying expectations and responsibilities for the master franchisee, so pay particular attention to what is expected of you and whether that aligns with your goals and background. Also pay attention to the length of the agreement and what happens after the agreement has expired. Do you have the option to renew the contract? Or does the franchisor take over your locations after a period of time?

With the right brand and the right candidate in place, master franchising can be a mutually beneficial opportunity. It also allows a franchisee to enjoy many of the financial perks usually afforded only to the franchisor.

While master franchising essentially allows the buyer to build their own franchise empire, financing is often difficult to obtain for this type of business as most of the investment is tied to intellectual property.

A master franchise investment can vary widely, from millions for an exclusive countrywide license with an established brand to as low as $100,000 for a small city with an emerging concept.

The ideal personality type for master franchising is someone who is outgoing and able to interact with a wide range of people, as you will be receiving franchise inquiries on a regular basis. You should be able to train, lead, and manage your group, as well as be committed to helping your franchisees, regardless of the situation. By making sure they are successful, particularly when they first open, you are likely securing yourself years of relatively passive income.

CHAPTER TWELVE – CONCLUSION

YES, YOU CAN LOSE EVERYTHING

We receive many calls and emails from ex-franchise owners thanking us for spreading the message regarding industry improprieties. There are also hundreds of comments on our YouTube videos from failed franchisees who were sold a bill of goods and ultimately lost a lot of money.

These hundreds of stories represent only a fraction of the investors whose franchise dreams eventually turned into a nightmare. According to the statistics, there are thousands more from which we will never hear.

Beyond the gag orders and non-disclosure agreements that buyers sign which restrict them from going public, many failed investors resign themselves to just turning the other cheek. To forget about the painful and costly lesson. And can they be blamed? Losing a lifetime of savings is a traumatizing event that ranks with the worst experiences one can have.

One recent story from a single mom of two autistic kids was particularly impactful. You can see our interview with her on our YouTube channel. She lost everything to a company that allegedly took her franchise away *after only 51 days*.

And by everything, we are talking three million dollars.

It took her four years to get the franchise open, but only 51 days for the franchise company to take the business away from her According to the now-broke-and-living-on-food-stamps ex-franchisee, she was even refused the option to resell her franchise, even if just to recoup a fraction of the investment.

Instead, the company took the franchise from her, then sold the business for pennies on the dollar to an existing owner in the system.

And based on the franchise agreement that the ex-franchisee signed, taking her business away was well within this franchise's legal rights.

When we spoke with the once-millionaire, now-penniless ex-franchisee, one statement she made was particularly poignant:

"If someone had advised me of these risks, I never would have invested."

And that is the problem. Buyers sign these complex legal documents after highly optimistic and jovial sales presentations, without understanding the possible repercussions if things go bad.

In our society, thinking about and weighing up potential negatives often means you're a downer. It's not how an entrepreneur should think! Even on our YouTube channel, we are advised continuously in the comments section that we are being "too negative" and should focus only on the positive outcomes.

But all investors should be aware of the risks. To ignore them is folly. Even before looking at franchises, buyers need to consider their own unique appetite for risk. And they need to consider the worst-case "what if" scenarios.

The franchisor won't talk much (if at all) about these risks. But you need to ask these questions.

"What happens if my franchise ultimately has to close?"

Are you allowed to resell the business? Are you responsible for ongoing royalties? And if so, how much will that be? Can *your spouse* also be on the hook for unpaid royalties if you are unable to pay them, even if they never signed the agreement? In certain states, that is a thing.

Unlike stocks, your risks could extend well beyond the initial amount you invested with a franchise. Through the liquidated damages clause, you could be liable for years of additional royalty fees, even if you close down. And even if it is through no fault of your own.

Some franchises have extremely low risk. Some have a higher risk and dismal failure rates. But none, not a single one, has zero risk.

Even for buyers back in 2019 who conducted thorough research and diligence, looking at every potential factor involved, risk was still there. Did anyone see Covid-19 coming? We certainly didn't. Subsequently, buyers who did all the right research got blindsided by a previously unknown virus that decimated businesses across the globe.

There is no way to eliminate risk entirely.

But the fact remains that we all need to do *something* with our money. Stocks, bonds, real estate investment trusts, precious metals, Bitcoin, or a franchise. We can't just bury our moolah in the backyard in a watertight-coffee can.

Even keeping our money "safe" in the bank is a risk as our savings continuously become eroded by inflation. And with record amounts of money, to the tune of trillions, being conjured from thin air, currency debasement is likely to get worse.

So unless we are OK with losing money every year to the ravages of inflation, we need to invest it somewhere.

As Robert Kiyosaki once said, "The biggest risk a person can take is to do nothing."

This statement becomes even more relevant in a world that is nearing 0% interest rates. The default setting of doing nothing today is a guaranteed loss of money every year.

Franchising, *for the right person* and in the right environment, can provide a solid investment vehicle. And risk can be minimized, but not eliminated. As a prospective investor, you need to be aware of all the risks and the potential outcomes if you do fail. You need to weigh and compare these risks with other financial opportunities. There is no universal right or wrong answer. Every investor's risk tolerance, local market demand, lifestyle goals, and other considerations will impact the decision.

There are thousands of happy franchise owners who have become enormously successful. But many also lost all of their money.

Success leaves clues, as does failure. Part of your due diligence should include determining whether those who did fail bear any resemblance to your own profile.

Are you buying a franchise that requires sales? Did the previous owners of many of the locations that closed come from engineering or accounting backgrounds? Are you an engineer or an accountant? Red flag. Higher risk.

In a food franchise situation, did the failed locations mostly have owners with no previous food experience? Do you have no food experience? Red flag. Higher risk.

There is a multitude of considerations far too vast to include in a single book. And frankly, first-time buyers shouldn't be expected to know all of these things.

Fortunately, as noted throughout these pages, you don't have to. Buyers in the USA or Canada are welcome to use any or all of our free tools, analysis, and coaching to help them uncover risks and determine the best options.

Tools such as the psychometric assessment, also available on the website, are valid anywhere in the world – feel free to use them!

A favorite quote of mine, which is attributed to Abraham Lincoln, is, "Give me six hours to chop down a tree and I will spend four sharpening my axe."

High-quality preliminary research into any investment will yield dividends. Unfortunately, much of the franchise industry wants buyers to invest quickly and make these decisions on emotion alone.

As we've explained in this book, any tactics that appear overly pushy or provide you only with positive information are a red flag.

Franchising is never a sure thing, but risks can be significantly reduced if researched appropriately and engaged with caution.

CONCLUSION

Could you help us spread this message? You might help save someone from financial disaster. We are just a small voice in a massive industry where a few big companies continue to mislead hundreds of unsuspecting buyers every year.

You can help us spread the word in a few quick and easy ways:

1. Leave us a review on Amazon or wherever you purchased this book
2. Leave us a review on our Facebook page https://www.facebook.com/pg/TheFranchiseCity/reviews/
3. Subscribe to our YouTube channel. There are also hundreds of videos on franchising and business which you may find helpful https://www.youtube.com/franchisecityonline

NEED HELP FINDING A FRANCHISE?

If you are considering buying a franchise and would benefit from following a proven, data-driven process and working with a franchise coach, Franchise City provides a comprehensive (free) service that helps franchise buyers avoid common mistakes and make better franchise buying decisions. You can learn more at:

https://www.franchise.city/our-services

ABOUT THE AUTHOR

Robert Edwards is an entrepreneur, investor, and franchising expert.

Robert also hosts the nation's most-watched YouTube channel on franchising and entrepreneurship, Franchise City Online, where he is best known for his hard-hitting critical franchise reviews.

https://www.youtube.com/franchisecityonline

Made in United States
Troutdale, OR
10/30/2024

24278120R00090